MARZIYA ZAKIRYANOVA

London, June 2014

LIFE OVER PAIN
AND
DESPERATION

HERTFORDSHIRE PRESS

Published in United Kindom
Hertforfshire Press Ltd © 2014

9 Cherry Bank, Chapel Street
Hemel Hempstead, Herts.
HP2 5DE, UK

e-mail: publisher@hertfordshirepress.com
www.hertfordshirepress.com

LIFE OVER PAIN AND DESPERATION
by **Marziya Zakiryanova**

First English edition

Recorded by Galia Shymyrbayeva
Translated by Bull Global Translation agency
Edited by Laura Hamilton

*British Library Catalogue in Publication Data
A catalogue record for this book is available from the British Library
Library of Congress in Publication Data
A catalogue record for this book has been requested*

ISBN 978-0-9927873-3-2

This book was written by someone on the brink of death. Her life had been split in two: before and after the first day of August 1991 when she, a mother of two small children and full of hopes and plans for the future, became disabled in a single twist of fate.

Narrating her tale of self-conquest, the author speaks about how she managed to hold her family together, win the respect and recognition of people around her and above all, protect the fragile concept of 'love' from fortune's cruel turns.

By the time the book was submitted to print, Marziya Zakiryanova had passed away. She died after making the last correction to her script.

We bid farewell to this remarkable and powerfully creative woman.

Unity, which proclaims the wisdom of our day,
Can be forged only by iron and blood.
But we shall try to forge unity with love,
Then we shall see which is the stronger.

Fyodor Tyutchev

FOREWORD

ONCE ALIVE,LEARN TO SURVIVE

When my old friend and colleague, Sergey Mikhaylovich Manakov, sent me a book written by his university friend, he asked only one thing of me: to read it and send him my impressions. I opened the untitled book and read the name of the author: Marziya Zakiryanova. Sergey had spoken about her often with great admiration but I had never met her. At that time, I still lived in Almaty, a city which I loved dearly. I had spent thirty three years of my life in Kazakhstan and felt spiritually and intellectually close to the country's people, their culture and their literature. I had even mastered the language well enough to translate Kazakh poetry.

I was excited by the prospect of reading this book especially since it had been co-authored by Marziya's husband, Kairat Zakiryanov who was also well respected by Sergey. All three, Sergey, Marziya and Kairat, were about the same age as me.

To say that this book belongs in the *must-read* category is an understatement. The wise, vibrant and poignant narrative is dedicated to a modest family and people close to the author yet the book has the capacity to reach out to a much wider audience. This is a guide to life but not only for those facing difficult situations. Here, you will find no irritating or tedious moral high ground. Instead, this is a story which focuses on the values afforded by living an honest and decent life.

Unfortunately, tragedy comes without warning. It is omnivorous and does not discriminate by age, nationality or anything else. And how should the victim respond? Should she embrace the changes and carry on with her life or give up and merely linger on? What if she, like Anna Akhmatova, were to make the bold resolution that she *must learn to live again*?

These questions like many others are candidly addressed by the authors with sincerity and honesty, often re-opening old wounds.

Marziya Zakiryanova was determined to learn how to live again and in so doing, taught people close to her how to appreciate life and all of its manifestations. Perhaps, some of the able-bodied amongst us will be tempted to dismiss this book as irrelevant but I would argue that its message applies to us all, regardless of our physical condition. One of its key messages concerns the importance of being able to raise your own expectations when faced with seemingly unbearable situations. Even if you are not directly afflicted, the problems faced by the author and the main characters in her story can emerge in any family. You are asked to appreciate how little can be achieved by someone if they are left all alone and at the same time, gain an understanding of how important it is to be surrounded and supported by parents, family , friends and of course, your children.

So what can a family do when one of their own suffers such a terrible blow? I think you would agree that when grief takes root and starts growing, it becomes very difficult for personal relationships to develop and continue as normal. Practicing tolerance, demonstrating benevolence and learning to forgive, all require significant spiritual strength and clarity of vision. As this book reveals, Marziya Zakiryanova possessed all of these traits and was thus able to spread love and selflessness to everyone close to her.

Reviewing a book is a challenging task and I would much prefer the role of a simple reader. My own life has not been a "walk in the park", and these days, it is certainly far from easy. Reading this unique creation I realized that overcoming unbearable torment requires the strength of a Titan. On a personal level, I am totally convinced by the philosophy outlined in this book. Looking back at my own life, I also wonder how I managed at times. What kind of power sustained me? It was only after reading this book that I was able to answer some of my own questions. I literally 'lived' through the book alongside the author and its main characters from the first to the last page, and I am eternally thankful to both Sergey Mikhailovich and his friends for providing me with that opportunity. I found that I had a lot in common with the main protagonist and remarkably, like Marziya, I too had a dog that was once poisoned by some evil souls. In her manuscript, the author refers to the very same writers and literature that were among my own role models: the poetry of Fyodor Tyutchev, Chingiz Aitmatov's explanation of Mankurtism *(mankurt: a slave tortured to the point of total memory loss, thereby becoming completely submissive)*, and Lermontov, who perished at a young age. Even the lyrics quoted by the author are the same as those which I received from a frustrated young man, back in my student years:

I shall not stoop before you.
Neither thy greeting, nor thy reproach
Has control over my soul.
Be aware that we are strangers from now on.

The issue of ethnicity is also one of my long-term interests and indeed, is something which causes me great concern especially when I hear it discussed on certain radio stations. Like Marziya, I have never understood the mind of the bigot which wills the destruction of other people and I thank the Lord for sparing me from this monster.

On more than one occasion I have had to overcome the treachery of people close to me and I know well, the desperation and total hopelessness of conditions experienced by disabled people in the nineties. Our pensions were often withheld for as long as six months and I was driven to taking sedatives in order to escape the hunger that chased me when I was awake.

I hope that this is something which I will never again have to endure. Yet, I sometimes feel that it is important that we remember such hardships, if only to avoid becoming *Mankurts*.

I finished this book in one sitting. Thank you my dear compatriots, for inviting me to step back into that distant, unforgettable time. Reading your book, I felt as though we were reliving our youth together : life in the students' halls, swapping rented rooms, descending upon cheap cafes with friends after receiving our monthly scholarship allowances, rushing to get to class on time, wandering the midnight streets of the city I loved so much, going to the theatre... And also fighting high-handed bureaucrats, the three-day ordeal to deliver my only child and as he grew, just like yourselves, searching for a better way of greasing the wheels in order to get him admitted to the kindergarten closest to my home.

However heart-rending its content; this book is a pleasure to read. The language is clear and modern yet its style remains classical. Despite the fact that the authors have retained the real names of the characters and described actual events, it reads like a novel. I believe that this book should be translated into other languages, beginning with Kazakh, so that it can reach the wide audience it deserves. I would even dare to advocate that this book provides a guide to the resolution of many universal issues.

Roza Akhtyamova,
Writer, poet and translator

WITH PAIN COMES WISDOM

Marziya Zakiryanova

This book is addressed to my descendants. I want to tell them a story of a happy woman who was their grandmother and great-grandmother...

The German philosopher and writer Kurt Vonnegut re-phrased a wise, oriental saying when he wrote: "Oh Lord, give me power to overcome what I can. Oh Lord, give me patience to survive what I cannot overcome. And Lord, give me wisdom to tell one from the other"...

It's not enough to merely survive; we must live our lives to the full, no matter what. Using my own life as an example I learnt that despite being confined to a wheelchair, there is far more to life than mere existence: you should love and be loved, support the career of your spouse, raise and enjoy your children and grandchildren and create a beautiful and secure home.

On the first day of August 1991 after the car accident, life as I knew it changed forever: a spinal injury had rendered me disabled. In October 2012, I was subsequently diagnosed with a terminal disease that consumes the body at a ferociously fast pace, sometimes within a few months. For me, the fight to combat cancer was a new phase of my life's trials. I don't know how other people would have responded but being a workaholic; this is where I found salvation. I decided to counter deadly thoughts by working on the book which friends and family had been encouraging me to write for some time.

I would like my children Baurzhan and Asel, my grandchildren, Tamerlan, Arslan, Tomiris, Ruslan and Donat, and in turn their children and grandchildren, to feel that they have a connection with the life of Marziya Zakiryanova. Most importantly, it is my wish that this biography of their mother and grandmother will help them to understand that every human life is priceless, poetic and interesting in all of its manifestations, including its unpredictability. And to all of them, and of course to my husband Kairat Zakiryanov, I would like to profess my love. I tried to be happy even when I was confined to a wheelchair and I succeeded in the name of my love for them. For all of that and my ability to overcome difficult circumstances, I give thanks. My life has become so rich, active and bright that not only my relatives but even I myself, often forget about the wheelchair.

I have included our family trees in this book, both mine and Kairat's, to ensure that our grandchildren are made aware of their origins.

Galiya Shimyrbaeva, the journalist who helped me write the book, asked me on several occasions about its intended audience: Was it for my family or the general public? We discussed this at length with Kairat and finally decided that we would only be able to answer that question when it was finished.

If the book were to appeal to people beyond my own family, it would become not only a memorial for my kin but also serve as a broader aid particularly for people with spinal disabilities, in the daily search for earthly joy.

It is my hope that my experiences of dealing with such blows of fate will help sufferers to overcome any feelings of inferiority and inspire people to lead good lives of which they can be proud. This would make me happy and I would rest in peace, assured that the precious time and energy spent writing this book in my current condition wasn't wasted. I have to confess that it has sometimes been very hard to revisit memories and difficult periods from the past but I feel that there are many people who need this to be done. Even my late mother, Sheshe, drew strength from my approach to life and once, when she was very ill, commented: 'Marziya, *aynalayin* (dear - Kazakh), if you can endure all of this, why can't I?'...

LIFE IS A GAME IN WHICH NO-ONE CAN PREDICT THE WINNERS OR THE LOSERS

Kairat Zakiryanov

After twelve years of marriage, we were still rambling about without a permanent roof over our heads; an unstable situation made worse by the fact that the woman from whom we rented a room could have asked us to pack up and leave at a moment's notice. We could therefore not have been happier than when we were allocated our own room in the Students' Residential Halls of the Ust-Kamenogorsk Pedagogical Institute.

My success in attaining my Candidate's thesis was in the best interest of my entire family. At that time, people with a Candidate of Science degree, equivalent to a Ph.D. Y1, were the elite and once they had obtained the title of Associate Professor they could earn 320 roubles per month in comparison to an 'ordinary' lecturer's wage of only 125. Thus, to spare me the worry of providing our daily bread, my wife assumed sole responsibility for supporting our family and secured a fairly prestigious job as a computer programmer with Vostokkazgeologiya.

When I became a Candidate in 1987, we continued to dwell in our room in the Student Halls. We were at the bottom of the queue of people waiting to get an apartment, but Erezhep Alkhairovich Mambetkaziev, Rector of the Pedagogical Institute, had his own methods of dealing with the housing issue. One day, he took me aside to tell me "It's almost the janitor's turn to get a flat, but his situation is uncertain and I am aware that if you, Zakiryanov, don't find better accommodation soon, you might decide to move to Almaty." He therefore arranged for me to jump the queue and get the apartment . At the time I was the only expert in algebra and numbers theory and not just in Ust-Kamenogorsk; there were only two or three of us in the whole of Kazakhstan! The Institute, known then as the Kirov Kazakh State University, was starved of teachers in my subject matter. I finally obtained my degree, we had an apartment and I was promoted to the position of Chair and later, Deputy Rector. Meanwhile, the kids were growing up and delighting us with their progress.

By then, I had become part of the Rector's inner circle. Erezhep Alkhairovich insisted that we, his pro-rectors, should remain at work until he left the office and because he used to work long hours, it was normal for us to stay until eight or nine in the evening. On one occasion, my colleagues appeared at my desk, having decided to share their observation that for an entire month, despite their spending every evening in the Rector's office, he never called up anyone apart from me. So we made a gentlemen's agreement that should anyone be needed, I would telephone one of them, and in five minutes that person would report to the Rector.

Luckily everyone, apart from me, lived close by.

One of my duties was to welcome all of the Rector's guests whenever they arrived from Almaty but at the same time, my family would be waiting for me at home. While supportive of my being detained by serious issues, my wife Marziya seemed unable to tolerate these other little trade-offs of my job and continuously grumbled about me coming home so late. I recall feeling irritated and thinking: "Why don't you understand that the well-being of our family is dependent on my career?"

Erezhep Alkhairovich, an ambitious man, had outgrown Ust-Kamenogorsk by the early 90's. It was clear that the position of Rector of a provincial Pedagogical Institute, which he had managed to turn into a University by 1991, was no longer quite enough for him. Like my teacher, I too had no lack of ambition.

By the summer of 1991, I was still a young man, but my career had risen from an ordinary teacher to pro-rector and I felt that I could achieve much more. I knew that if Erezhep Alkhairovich was promoted to a position in Almaty, he would most probably recommend me for Rector. However, even the Rector's position, which was within easy reach, didn't tempt me much. It is only now that I understand that being a good Rector is better than being a mediocre Minister, who is likely to be forgotten within a year or two of leaving the Board. But back then it was assumed that a ministerial position was a mandatory attribute of any successful career: a situation which predominated in an era when any capable candidate had the opportunity to rise to a position of great power, with or without influential friends and wealth.

My wife had plans of her own. In early 90's, when money and housing were no longer a problem, she dreamt of realising her own professional aspirations. She had already earned a reputation as a respected system programmer in Ust-Kamenogorsk and was also highly valued in Novosibirsk, where she had worked in a computer centre whilst I concentrated on my thesis. She could easily have embarked on a scientific career and obtained a degree. Had that happened, Marziya, with her analytical mind and brilliant organizational skills, would have risen to the position of Head of research or an educational institution by now. And as for the children, like most parents, we planned to secure a top class education for them in one of the Universities of Almaty, Moscow or St-Petersburg.

THE CITY WHERE EVERYTHING BEGAN

The enjoyment of wandering about my own home on my own two feet was not to last: just four years later my body would be broken and I would need to adjust to my new physical condition and the changes in lifestyle which came with it.

After Kairat had been awarded his degree of Associate Professor, we moved to his hometown, despite options of going to other cities including Aktyubinsk, where I come from. The Pedagogical Institute where he enrolled as a teacher provided us with a large room of 17.5 square metres in the Student Halls. Sparsely furnished, all that it contained were four single, steel beds, three built-in closets and a table. At the earliest opportunity we purchased a kitchen table, four stools, a white buffet and, if I recall correctly, a nightstand. I also brought several second-hand book shelves from Novosibirsk. Later when we, as a teaching staff family, received a two-room suite on the third floor, I built an additional bookcase but even then, there was not enough room for all of our books. Our family moved into this apartment in my absence since our trade union had arranged for me to go to the sanatorium for treatment for a gastric ulcer. By the time I returned, Kairat and his friends had already assembled all of the furniture.

Naturally, having our own apartment was a dream come true! Every night, when the children were asleep (it was an ironclad rule that they were in bed by nine thirty on school nights), I walked from room to room. I still couldn't believe that this spacious apartment of 85 square metres was ours! My feelings during those moments were even more intense than when I heard that we'd finally got the apartment: Freedom at last!

After we moved to Ust-Kamenogorsk, it took quite a while to get a job which matched my profile. During the Soviet era this city, located in the East of the Republic, had strong ties with Moscow. The head offices of the giants of the base metals industry, including VNIItsvetmet, UMZ, STsK and TMK, were all located here. In terms of supplies, from food to human resources, there were special allowances and almost all of the employees, from engineers and technical staff down to the factory workers, were Slavic.

I do not know the purpose of this policy. It was based perhaps, on a requirement for high qualifications and specialist experience, or a government order not to employ or promote local people. The latter seems more likely: well-trained technical specialists from the local community were available but somehow they were never accepted for employment in these enterprises.

I myself had experienced such discrimination. Before Kairat obtained his science degree, his salary was could not cover all of our expenses, so I applied for a well-paid job worthy of my high qualifications. When employed by the Novosibirsk Research Institute of Software Systems I was promoted to senior engineer-programmer within two years and had also completed a two-month capacity building programme in Leningrad. Yet, looking for job in the computing centres of local enterprises proved fruitless: all of my applications were rejected, despite a universal shortage of programmers. So, determined not to waste any more time, I enrolled at the local branch of the Kazakh Polytechnic Institute as a teacher of advanced mathematics.

After a while, I managed to secure a job in the computing centre of Vostokkazgeologiya where I was the only Kazakh amongst Russians, Jews and Germans. I worked in this organization until I got a job at the Road Construction Institute. By that time, Kairat had already completed his thesis and had been promoted to pro-rector. This meant that our material difficulties were more or less resolved and most importantly, Asel had started going to school close to our home. Previously, we had to take two buses to get her to kindergarten from our home district CShT, named after the locally based Combined Silk Textiles works, and I barely made it to my office on time.

In other words, all was going well apart from the usual, incidental problems which affect any family. We had roof over our heads, the children were growing up and we enjoyed the company of our friends. My leisure hours were filled with physical activities and I also encouraged the children to enjoy sport and the outdoors. Although there were always plenty of things to do around the house at the end of the working week, I tried my best to take them out of town on either Saturday or Sunday.

Asel was only three when I bought her a tiny pair of skis. There was ski route near the Pedagogical Institute, running alongside the Komendantka River. I often rose before dawn to bake buns and prepare lunch, ready for us all to go skiing in the morning. Vostokkazgeologiya often provided buses to take staff to the countryside. In the winter, we would sledge and ski down the slopes and in the spring, summer and autumn; everyone enjoyed walking, playing and sharing picnics.

In Almaty, I skated a lot and although ice rinks were less common in Ust-Kamenogorsk, I bought skates for the kids anyway. I felt that their physical development and well-being were just as important as everything else and I was therefore delighted when Baurzhan, in addition to building model aeroplanes, ships and yachts at the Young Technicians Station, took up Thai-kwoon-do. I must admit, however, that standing at the window waiting for him to come home at nine or ten at night, caused me a great deal of anxiety and I'm now surprised that I allowed such a young boy to make his own way to and from the classes.

It would be an exaggeration to say that I was heavily immersed in all aspects of my children's lives but I was always involved with their progress at school. People tend to assume that teachers can teach everything, providing both knowledge and the fundamentals of ethics. I do not share this belief. Parents must know what's happening in the hearts of their children and what are they are thinking about. Kairat also spent a lot of time with the kids, playing or talking to them, but it was me who dealt with their day-to-day affairs and most importantly, the spiritual aspect of their lives.

By the time I got back in the evenings, the kids were already at home and if dinner was not ready, they were summoned to help. The younger one was given potatoes to wash whilst the elder was entrusted with a knife to peel them. Needless to say, Baurzhan was already able to cook at the age of seven. Sometimes, when I came home for lunch, he would proudly announce that he had made chips all by himself. Cooking with six hands is not just faster, it had another specific purpose. When the kids were busy preparing the meals or cleaning the rooms, I chatted to them about school.

My questions encouraged my children to try and recall what they had learned in their classes. As a result, even before starting their homework they had revised what they had studied that day. At the same time, rather than being a formal exercise, it provided conversation laced with plenty of smiles, laughs and jokes. To keep conversation flowing in both directions, I often told them what was happening at my work. If you talk to children as if they are adults, they are less likely to kill time fooling around and tend to grow more self-confident. Most importantly, it helps the parent to build and maintain a spiritual connection with them.

I maintained a spiritual connection with my husband as well. Our relationship was not perfect – we both have explosive tempers- but we were a family. I remember times when as I was doing something at home, he would describe in great detail, a book he had just finished. He would also try to talk me into buying new books, despite the fact that we could barely afford it. I loved reading as much as my husband but it was up to me to take care of both Kairat and our children and you can't fill your stomach with books! At the time, Kairat did not involve himself with domestic issues and although he loved me and his heart had always belonged to the family, worrying about what we would eat or how we would buy clothes, only came to him much later. It could be said that he only "grew-up" after turning fifty, when he finally realized that the family needed his attention.

However, I do admit that full credit for procuring our apartment goes to Kairat. Erezhep Alkhairovich Mambetkaziev, Rector of the Pedagogical Institute, later named the East Kazakhstan State University, recognized the true value of Kairat's teaching and managerial talents.

What united us then and continues to unite us now, is our shared intolerance for hypocrisy; both in personal relationships and in the expression of thought. Tamerlan, our elder grandson, in a poem which he dedicated to our wedding anniversary, correctly noted that we "loved each other, although we fought again and again". Yes, we argue a lot. It happens that I have my own opinion on everything and I, as a mathematician, have to find a logical correlation and apply it to almost everything. That is why I'm never bored; there's always something worth contemplating. This could be small issues related to daily life or larger issues, concerning ethics, spirituality or morality.

Relationships with our extended family fell into the latter category. I never fought with Kairat over my relatives but we had disputes, as if I were their enemy, over his. Perhaps this was because I used to voice my thoughts openly to whomever they applied. When I was dying in intensive care after the accident, I was saved by Talgat, Kairat's younger brother. Later on, whenever we got involved in fierce arguments with him about some particular situation or other, my husband's relatives tried to shame me by saying: "you must forgive him, for after all and you've said it yourself, he saved your life!" Of course I am grateful to him and appreciate the level of professionalism which he showed when he was still a young doctor but that doesn't mean that I have to agree with everything he says and does.

But I am straying from my story. By the early nineties, I was seriously thinking about submitting my own thesis. To build a career in higher education (by then, I had spent the last few years working in Advanced

Mathematics at the Road Construction Institute), a scientific degree was a necessity. Obviously, my age prohibited me from progressing towards more in- depth mathematical research and following Kairat's path. Having recognized early on that his capacity for research surpasses mine and that his career should focus on science, I had no hesitation in lowering my own ambitions.

Being a decent engineering programmer, I always managed to secure well-paid jobs. At least, my salary allowed us to lead a decent life providing enough to both buy books and raise the children. Later, when we moved into the apartment and Kairat became Pro-Rector, I could afford to move to a less well-paid job that allowed me more time for the family.

When I finally decided to opt for a career in science, I was offered a choice of research subjects including mathematical teaching methodology and acmeology, which was a new scientific discipline for studying problems of personal development and professional growth. I had already started selecting literature and was making plans for how I would combine working on my thesis with my job, caring for the family and visiting my research tutor in Moscow or St Petersburg…

This is what my life was like up until 1st August 1991

RENDEZVOUS WITH FATE

Kairat Zakiryanov

Everything came crumbling down on one day: August 1ˢᵗ, 1991.

My father had passed away in April of that same year. He had suffered hardships and adversities but at the same time, people and events had made his life   remarkably rich. On his deathbed he asked for a tall mazar with a soaring and airy blue dome to be erected over his grave.

While on business trips to various regions of Kazakhstan, I took the opportunity to check out Muslim cemeteries. One day, returning from Semipalatinsk and driving through the small town of Charsk, I noticed a mazar of an unusual shape. It looked similar to what my father described and by asking the locals, I discovered that it had been created by a builder named Nikolay Shukhov. I sought him out and we agreed to have the mazar constructed by the end of July. As soon as our University had finished processing applications for the following academic year, I took Marziya and the kids to the village where I grew up and in Karakul, paid a final tribute to my father by laying the foundation bricks of his mazar. Our stay was brief and we had only two or three days before we had to hurry back home to Ust-Kamenogorsk. On the first of August we were expecting a visit from Professor Zhdanov, my colleague and our rector's friend and teacher. He was arriving from Moscow to visit the lake of Markakol and I was going to accompany him. We could have taken a bus or hired a car but I did something for which Marziya still reproaches me: I called Aleksandr Ivanovich Fedosov, a friend of mine who was deputy chairman of the Ispolkom District and member of the Executive Committee of the Communist Party. He readily responded to my request for a private car, as I knew he would and I must admit that I looked forward to showing off to my relatives, what a hot-shot I had become!

So we headed out to meet our fate. It transpired that the driver provided by the Committee was totally inexperienced, having only gained his license the week before. I took the front seat beside him and my wife, kids and Fedosov's two daughters sat in the back. As we passed the village of Tayinty, only 80 kilometres from the city, it started raining. Up ahead was a bread delivery truck parked at the side of the narrow road but just as our UAZ was about to pass the damn truck, its driver decided to get out of the cab! We were in danger of running him over so our novice driver yanked the car to the left, causing the car to skid over the slippery verge and then tumble down the steep slope on the other side! I regained consciousness in response to being slapped on the cheeks and heard my daughter desperately calling: "Daddy, Daddy!" I was soaked in blood and the pain was so severe that I wished I were already dead. Marziya was lying a bit further away. She wasn't bleeding but showed no signs of life. However, we managed to bring her round and she tried to speak. We had no idea that she had suffered a spinal trauma as we pulled her from under the wreckage and carried her towards the road to wave down a passing car.

Then ill fate struck again! If only we had been able to get a lift to the regional centre, the outcome of my wife's accident would have been so much better. At this stage, Marziya still had control of her feet and she would definitely have recovered, had she been operated on immediately. However, none of the cars going towards Ust-Kamenogorsk stopped and so our only hope was to accept a lift in a Lada which was travelling in the opposite direction. I asked the driver to take us to the nearest hospital which was located in the village of Asubulak. We laid Marziya on the back seat and I sat with her head on my knees. The kids, Baurzhan and Asel, sat in the front next to the driver.

In the village hospital they injected Marziya with a painkiller and I called Talgat, my younger brother who was an emergency doctor in intensive care at the regional hospital. Due to the rain, they were unable to send a helicopter for Marziya, so my brother drove to us in an ambulance with the surgeon, V. Terentenko. However, since there was an inadequate supply of blood, they decided that surgery would be too risky.

We stayed at a hotel for the night. In the morning, the helicopter finally made it and Marziya was taken into theatre at the regional hospital that evening. But once again, fate proved merciless: the surgeon, either drunk or suffering from a bad hangover incorrectly fastened the screws of the metal plates holding together the broken bone. As a result, the plates became detached, causing severe swelling over Marziya's back. And so my wife had to undergo another operation, and then another and another...

Within ten days I was made aware of the gravity of her condition but as yet, Marziya knew nothing. Our surgeons summoned their colleagues from the neurosurgical centre in the capital. After examining my wife and studying her x-rays, the expert from Almaty called me in and warned me that I should prepare myself for bad news: from that day forth my wife would need to adjust to being confined to a wheelchair. My mind was a blur as I left the doctor's office. I called Zhenis Sadykov, Dean of the new medical department at our university. He refused to believe that Marziya, so active, lively and sport-loving, would never be able to walk again. He tried to console me up by telling me that modern medical science had made significant advances and that some kind of treatment would soon be available. ... I couldn't bear to tell Marziya about her diagnosis. She had to wait for four months to be 'enlightened' by our 'soviet' doctor. Examining her at home, our district neuropathologist presented her with the shocking news: "Forget about standing up, lady, you'll be lucky if you are even able to take care of yourself". I wasn't at home at the time, but I can imagine what impact this had on my wife. Up until then, her spirit had been sustained by hope but that evening, as I crossed the doorstep, she said in a dull voice devoid of emotion: "I no longer want to live."

I am ashamed to admit that unable to control my emotions, I yelled that while dying might seem like the easy option for her, who would be left to raise our children? And what would happen to me?! Startled, Marziya regained her self-control but the depression which had engulfed her didn't pass. I was always aware of it, despite her efforts to suppress and hide it deep within her.

My wife then ordered me to buy a return ticket for her sister.

The moment that Marziya refused the help of relatives, was the moment she started a totally new life.

I RETURN FROM THE DEAD

After gaining his degree, Kairat continued to visit his research advisor in Novosibirsk but by using computer- assisted calculations, I was able to help with some of the problems which arose as he struggled with work on his theorem.

In general, I found programming both interesting and highly stimulating but it could also prove quite frustrating. In addition to knowledge of computer languages, it requires logical and analytical thinking, otherwise the merciless machine keeps feeding you messages about your errors as if to say: "You've still got a lot to learn, my dear!" You continually feel as though you are fighting on two fronts: one against yourself and the other, against thinking apparatus.

It proved to be exhausting work and I felt depleted by the time I got home. However, there was no time to sit and relax for even fifteen minutes. By evening, our two rooms in the halls looked as though they had been hit by a hurricane. Blankets and sheets hung down from tables, evidence that Asel and our neighbours' girls had been making dens, and it was obvious that Baurzhan had also had his friends round...

I ended up going to bed very late at night. Life wasn't easy for women in the Soviet era. It was difficult to source even the most basic commodities and washing and darning children's clothes was part of the daily routine, alongside cooking three meals a day. Rising at five-thirty, I had to make breakfast, get the children ready for school and be out of the door by seven to make it to work by eight. The main reason for resigning from the Vostokkazgeologiya computer centre was to get home earlier!

When I began teaching at the Road Construction Institute, I had to re-familiarize myself with the basics of the advanced math's course: mathematic analysis, analytical geometry and probability calculus, and since there wasn't a job for me on the Maths degree course during my first year at RCI, I had to spend that year teaching elementary mathematics to students on pre-entry courses.

Once, not long before the life-changing accident, Kairat had to go on a trip to inspect student construction brigades which had been formed in the spring of 1989 to help with rebuilding after a major earthquake in Eastern Kazakhstan. As he was preparing for his journey I reminded him that back in 1975, when I was considering his proposal, he had promised me a zibeline coat within five years, and within ten years, to "throw the world at my feet". By then, fifteen years had passed and I teased: "Well, the coat never materialized, not to mention the world, so can you at least show me your homeland in Eastern Kazakhstan?" He could not deny me that, so in the summer of 1990 our family embarked on our first long journey.

On one of those days in the steppes of Tarbagatay district, we stopped our car by a natural spring. Another truck was already there, with a dozen young men standing around it. One of them walked up to me, saying: "Hello, Marziya Nurtazovna!" I recognized him instantly: he was an 'Afghani' *(a veteran of the Soviet campaign in Afghanistan),* and a student from my foundation course. Guys like him were considerably weaker at maths than the other students, but were highly motivated by the need to attain a good education. Knowing what kind of hell these lads had gone through in Afghanistan, filled with bloodshed, fear and death, I tried particularly hard to teach them.

Many of the other teachers, who had little interest in encouraging these guys, would simply award them a minimum score, or a 'pass', out of clemency. I on the other hand, pushed them quite hard towards an understanding of the logic of mathematics and was touched by how diligently they tried to grasp the subject. That's why I also helped the 'Afghanis' in exams, feeling that the experience they had received in that terrible war was in fact worth many high school degrees. I hoped that my other students would likewise understand. The guy we met near that spring thanked me by saying: "You were very strict but in retrospect, we were grateful to you for being so." To this day, I regard his appreciation of my work and efforts to be my most valuable reward.

That summer, we visited all corners of Eastern Kazakhstan and found the natural landscape glorious! On previous summer holidays, we had visited the Bukhtarminsk water reservoir using tickets provided by our trade union; sometimes we travelled by bus and sometimes, by motorboat. At that time, recreation zones didn't have many facilities–cabins offered nothing more than a bed and a mattress- so the holidaymakers had to bring along everything, including ten days' rations. Yet, these small discomforts couldn't spoil our family holidays in those happy years. We spent our days swimming, hiking and hunting for berries, mushrooms and of course, firewood. In the evenings we cooked on the bonfire and made jam from the berries; wild currant and raspberry, to sweeten the smoke-flavored tea.

The children kept the fire alive while their dad sang for us. Just as a small note: when Kairat was courting me, one of his advantages over his competitors was his singing talent. As for myself, I can't sing and because of that, hold in very high regard those who can. At half past nine we would send the children to bed and Kairat and I would stay up until one in the morning, sitting beside the bonfire on the shores of the Bukhtarminsk "sea", chatting or reading poetry to each other.

Those days were so wonderful that even today their memory fills my heart with joy. We were young, in love and delighted in our beautiful children. We didn't have a very large or close circle of friends at that time but when shooting a film about our family in 2011, Kairat pointed out that we were never bored with each other since there was always something to talk about. How true! As I write, my mind finds itself transported back to the bonfire, sitting in Kairat's close embrace as we watch sparks flying up into the dark, star-speckled skies.

That was how we spent our time at the Bukhtarma, but in the summer of 1990 we went to the Rakhmanov Springs. Many people refer to Katon-Karagay as 'another Switzerland'. In Europe however, while nature is touched by the human hand, Katon is an example of primordial, divine beauty! The snow-capped summit of Mount Belukha, much loved by climbers and clearly visible from the springs, provided a majestic backdrop as we soaked in hot radon baths during that unforgettable summer. Sadly these days, even if I were able to get to the springs, my health would prevent me from bathing and indeed, too much radon is not recommended for anyone.

We then travelled towards Lake Markakol. Despite being excited by the legendary beauty of the lake, if I had known in advance how difficult the road was, I would probably have refused to go. Back then, there only mountain tracks and neglected country roads and at times, it felt as if our Niva was rearing upwards, rather than sitting on the surface of the road itself. It was so scary! But eventually, after a long and steep ascent, we reached the hamlet of Urunkhaika where we were rewarded by a vision of heaven on earth: from every aspect were views of the vast expanse of the lake in its all its splendor, set against mountains crowned by white peaks!

It was August, and officially still summertime, but it was so cold up there that we didn't even think of swimming. Instead, Zarylkhan Mukhamadiev, Head of the Zaisansky district police department, and his wife Arai, took us fishing on the lake. This remarkable couple became our close friends and we have spent many happy times together. Although we live in different cities, our relationship with them remains as fresh as it was in our youth.

I have never seen such crystal-clear water as that in Markakol; not even in Temir, the river of my childhood home, or in Bukhtarma. Every single pebble and every fish on the riverbed was visible. We found ourselves immersed in a silent landscape, mesmerized by the glimmering water which stretched towards a horizon fringed by dark forestry.

The effort involved in reaching the lake could be justified alone by the flavours of the soup made from our fresh catch of lenok and grayling, and the walks in the forest proved equally magical. Berries grew in such abundance that we had no choice but to walk right over them. It reminded me of Novosibirsk, where I often embarked on bicycle trips with friends, camping in tents and gathering berries and mushrooms. Yet whilst everywhere in Novosibirsk seemed well trodden, this was a true wilderness which could sometimes feel quite threatening, especially when we could hear the sounds of animals close by.

When we stepped ashore after our fishing trip, we noticed a few lean-tos and a small gathering of people. We also noted several wooden barrels containing and strewn with berries, mushrooms and smoked fish. The group turned out to be three friends from Almaty (I remember that one had worked in the Alatau resort) who spent their annual holidays at Markakol. They had removed all of the seats from their Volgas, apart from the drivers', and filled all available space with gifts from nature. These city dwellers didn't fancy going to the beaches of Ibiza or the Bahamas since for them, nothing could beat the beauty of the shores of Lake Markakol. Similarly, my admiration of this land was so huge that we made a firm resolution to return with our family the following year.

There were, however, many unexpected changes in our lives before that next summer. Kairat's father became very ill. He was admitted to hospital in November and in April, passed away. After the dome had been erected over the father's grave in the last days of July, we were supposed to return to Ust Kamenogorsk and then embark on a trip to Markakol a day or two later. Our Rector's friends from Moscow, Stepan Ivanovich Zhdanov along with his son, and Fedor Ivanovich Lobanov, planned to accompany us. After hearing our stories they too wanted to see the natural sanctuaries of Eastern Kazakhstan.

I remember every minute of that day. We hurried to get to the city before dusk in order to buy food for the trip. I was planning, amongst other things, to drop by our dacha in Samsonovka to collect fruit and other stuff which we grew there. Before leaving, Kairat and the children went to his father's grave whilst I made some small repairs to his mother's house. Before leaving, Kairat told me to call the Deputy Chairman of the Samarsky District and ask him to send a car to pick us up at two o'clock in the afternoon.

I can't call it a premonition, but for some reason, I didn't want to do any of that and suggested instead: "If Marat (Kairat's older brother) drove us to the station, we could get a bus from there". But Kairat insisted that I made the phone call and I gave in. Unfortunately, the Deputy Chairman Fedosov was available...

We then had lunch with the men who were building the mazar and before climbing into the car; I spoke to the master-craftsman as he was sitting with a cigarette on the *zavalinka* (an extended footing attached to the wall of a house to protect it from freezing): "Thank you Nikolay, we're moving out; remember me kindly". Even now I can't explain where these words which very unusual for me, came from.

I remember that we stopped near a spring that ran by the road. How could I have ever imagined that this was the last time that I would ever walk along a path to get water on my own two feet? We set off again. The road was steep and I sat Asel on my knees and held her tightly. I had spent my childhood in the plain steppes and the hairpin bends of the mountains always gave me a thrill. After we had passed through the mountains and the road straightened out, I sat Asel by my side.

It started to rain and up ahead, we saw a bread delivery truck. It stopped, the door opened and the driver stepped out of the cabin. Our driver, afraid of hitting him, turned the wheel sharply and our car somersaulted off the elevated highway and down the steep grass verge.

… I can't recall the very moment of the crash –probably due to my body's protective mechanisms kicking in.

…I woke up briefly as I was being pulled into someone's car… We were then speeding along a rough road and obviously, the vibrations caused me a great deal of pain. I was aware of my own moans and Asel's voice as my daughter wept and cried out to the driver: "Careful! Careful! My mum is hurt!" When we arrived at the hospital, the surgeon or neurologist tested my sensitivity by running a tool against the skin of my feet. I felt it. He ordered that I move my fingers and I did…

And then, that was it: I passed out. No, there's one more moment I remember. I was lying on a stretcher, either in a corridor or in the ward. Kairat bent over me and called – "Marziya, Marziya… I won't be long: I'm just going to run off for a minute to check on the kids. They're here, with our relatives".

Later, my husband told that I kept asking, even when I wasn't fully conscious: "Kairat, don't leave me, don't walk away. If you go, I'll die."

Although he too had suffered a spinal compression fracture, he stayed on his feet until my situation was clear. A medical helicopter arrived in the morning but I don't remember that. I had undergone surgery during the night. Someone later told me that the entire operating room was splattered with blood: while operating, the semi-sober surgeon had severed a major artery. During those critical moments, Kairat paced back and forth below the hospital windows and despite being a self -professed atheist, begged the Lord: "Whatever her condition when she gets out of hospital, please just let her live!" "Why didn't you ask Him to return me to the state I was in before the accident, rather than put me in a wheelchair?" – I reproached him afterwards, half-serious, half-joking. Sadly, he replied: "I was afraid we'd get nothing, if I asked for too much".

I spent two weeks in a coma in intensive care. Almost all of my organs had failed and I was sustained by artificial lungs and a dialysis machine. I was saved by Talgat, Kairat's brother. An emergency physician, he worked in another hospital, but he was allowed to treat me. Seeing my marble-pale face he sounded a major alarm. After one more X-ray, they found that two broken ribs had pierced my lungs, causing a pulmonary hemorrhage. I remember a piercing pain under my right armpit as someone dug and poked around with a sharp instrument…

They pumped out almost two litres of blood from my lungs, adding to the serious amount of blood which I had lost of during surgery. According to Cocker, I should have departed this world and the doctors agreed that I had quite literally, returned from the dead.

During my two weeks of unconsciousness I was "visited" by my deceased grandmother. When she entered the room, I saw myself laid out on a high stretcher; it was as though I were looking down at myself from a high vantage point. Dressed in a long gown and holding a candle, Ani walked around me to my right, and then, without closing the circle on my left, walked towards exit. It was so clear that I do not have the heart to say it was a dream. This vision came to me shortly before I emerged from my coma.

I had another vision very recently, when my mother passed away. On 18 December of 2012 I awoke at five in the morning suffering from apnea. I pulled myself up to recover my breath. Kairat woke up and asked anxiously: "Marziya, what's happened?" I replied: "Sheshe's (*mother's*) body temperature has dropped to 32 degrees," "What are you talking about? Who told you? Did someone call you from Temir?" – "No," – "Maybe it was a dream, then?" – "No, it was not a dream." As I spoke, I frantically tried to figure out where I'd got this information from. I regained my breath, had my blood pressure, temperature and sugar level tested, then sipped a little water and calmed down a bit. We decided that it was a side-effect of my medication: I had finished my most recent course of chemotherapy less than a week before.

But at eight o'clock in the morning the phone rang and I knew even before answering it, that it was news about the death of my mother. I later learnt that she had passed away at exactly the same time that I had awoken with apnea.

STAYING ALIVE

Returning to the day when I came round after the accident: Only Kairat, who had been admitted to the floor above mine with a compression fracture and concussion, had permission to enter the recovery room. Struggling to gather my thoughts after such a long period of unconsciousness, I asked him to bring my cosmetics and a book of selected poems by Tyutchev. The first, I realised, would make me feel more feminine and more like an ordinary human being. My choice of Tyutchev was a more informed decision, based on my admiration for this poet's depth and wisdom. Whenever times were particularly difficult, I would even transcribe some of his lines and hang them in the kitchen where I spent much of my time. "The day is done, and thank God!" wrote the poet and these simple words were completely in tune with my inner spirit as I braced myself to endure yet more challenging situations.

On more than one occasion, I also found inspiration in the novel "«Gone with the Wind» and was especially drawn to one of Scarlett's favourite expressions: "I'll see about it tomorrow".

This is one of the best ways of achieving something when doubt and pain weaken both your ability to make immediate decisions or worse, dilute your desire to continue living. By postponing decision making, you allow time for contemplation and then come to realise that everything is not as gloomy as it first appeared.

I didn't read "Gone with the Wind" until I was an adult but I had lived according to this expression of Scarlett's since childhood. If I was unable to solve a problem, I defined the goal and then went to bed so that my sub -consciousness could work out an answer as I slept.

When I asked Kairat to bring the volume by Tutchev, I didn't realise what had happened to me and what the future held. I remember very well these early days, down to the smallest detail, but find it hard to describe them. Somewhere in the back of my mind I was aware that there was something very wrong with me. My relatives were sad and would not meet my eyes and I was given books on the subject, affording the doctors an indirect means of informing me of my poor condition.

Feeling as though half of my body had been dislocated or cast in cement was an awful and frightening experience and I constantly and hopelessly, tried to move my legs to dislodge the heavy weight pressing down on them. In addition, I had problems with my pelvis, bowels and kidneys.

When Kairat learnt from the Consultant from Almaty that I would be unable to walk, he couldn't face me. He was afraid that when I saw his eyes I might realise that there was nothing left to fight for.

Kairat's aunts, Raufa-apay and Khurma-apay, both doctors well informed in new developments in medical science, discovered an article in a Science and Life journal which had been written by a man named Dikul. In it, he outlined how he had developed special apparatus and managed to train his body to perform certain functions after he had become paralysed: there were also accounts of how he had demonstrated these re-acquired physical skills in public. Moreover, Dikul asserted that the human spirit is able to overcome all obstacles.

A second article however, entitled "Life at the Bottom" written by Leonid Krasov a young doctor paralysed by a ski-ing accident, related how attempts to follow these methods had failed to restore his health and as a result, he had become confined to a wheelchair. I tried to accept the fact that in all likelihood, a similar destiny awaited me. But my heart and every cell of my body railed against this reality and I wailed and cried "I cannot live like this!"

I was in hospital from August 1 to October 23 1991 and my relatives were constantly at my side. My mother had arrived in Ust-Kamenogorsk on the night of the accident and took immediate charge of the housekeeping and childcare. Thanks to her, Kairat strapped up in a corset, was able to return to work within a month. He managed to visit me in hospital three times a day at breakfast, lunch and dinner and since then, this has become the norm every time I am admitted to hospital. My sister Naziya arrived from Almaty with her two year old daughter , leaving her husband and son at home, and Torim, my second sister came from Aktubinsk, generously taking leave of her work to be near me. Joined by Kairat's sisters, Janna and Almaniya, they took it in turns to care for me twenty-four hours a day.

They turned me over at regular intervals and smoothed my sheets to prevent my getting bedsores . They also took care of any intestinal discharge and helped me to urinate, an essential act especially since my bowels had failed along with my liver and kidneys. At this point I couldn't even move my arms. I was forced to eat cucumber spread with caviar, having been advised that this was supposedly a good remedy for both the stomach and exhausted organs.

Everyone has problems with their health now and again but there is a particular hopelessness which overcomes someone whose spine has been broken. I may have been reproached in the early days for being over pessimistic but as a young wife and mother of two children, everything in my life had been thrown off balance and I had completely lost my sense of perspective. Anyone faced with such a situation needs to sort things out mentally and decide what they have to live for. When I learnt that I wouldn't be able to walk I made a clear plan: if fate allows me life then I should embrace both it and the needs of those who depend on me : my children! The key points in our existence, birth and death, are ordained by a supreme force and no human being has the right to assume this role, especially since taking one's own life has such an enormous and negative impact upon the destinies of children and relatives, forever bound to the perpetrator's sin. And I couldn't bear to imagine how my children would cope with having to admit that their mother had taken her own life. I recognised too, that if I refused to carry my burden it would not only be a manifestation of my weakness but also, a demonstration of protest against God. Hence, my response to the question of why I should continue living was both simple and complicated . You could say that the responsibilities of bringing up my children and keeping the home fires burning should have been enough to make life worth living but at first, it was the children who helped me rather than the other way round, so this was not the only reason for my carrying on. I accepted that if I had no right to die then I should strive to live my life with as much dignity as any able-bodied person . Instead of being pitied, I needed to rejoin the world of the able-bodied on equal terms and indeed, this turned out to be quite possible.

At the end of August 1991 Naziya was sent home and at the beginning of May 1992 Torim joined her with all my thanks for her help. Only my mother remained, looking after my children whilst I spent two months at the clinic in Saky, Crimea. In September she returned to Temir and was very disappointed that her grandson, my brother's child, had started his first year in High School without her being there.

And then the day came when we were left alone. The children had completely spurned any further services of housekeepers or assistants and I had learnt how to move myself from my bed to my wheelchair. Step by step,with the support of my children, I slowly began to manage the housekeeping myself.

My first attempts at moving around independantly, were difficult. There was no-one at home and I had to prepare lunch for my children while they were at school. Unable to reach the bag of potatoes, I tried to find a stick to help me but all this effort cost me dear and for the rest of that day, I could hardly move from my wheelchair.

Cleaning proved to be another challenge but if I put the bucket and mop against the footboard of my wheelchair, I devised a way of washing the floors: a process which gave me great satisfaction since I couldn't stand all the dust and mess! I arranged the furniture in such a way that I could move freely in my wheelchair to reach every nook and cranny. No special adaptations were made to our apartment since I refused to live in an environment which reminded me of being in hospital. The only outward sign of my disability was my wheelchair and everyone got so used to it that they soon took no notice of it.

I'm trying to describe all of this to illustrate that if someone really wants to do something, then they will achieve their goal. You must admit to yourself that there is alternative solution to the problem, and my own efforts were greatly sustained by the desire not to be a burden to my relatives , like some old heavy suitcase without a handle!

Step by step , we all adapted to our new way of life. One day, when the weather turned cold and damp, I experienced such pain that I had to lie down. Baurzhan and Aselya decided to cook borscht. It took them a whole day and in the evening when we sat down at the table, the children admitted that the experience of making the soup, a lengthy and complicated process, had made them appreciate all the more, the meals which I usually prepared for them. From that day onwards and over time, both became very proficient cooks!

In the early nineties our country was inundated with negative influences from abroad: prostitution, hard drinking and drugs. Many people were unable to protect their children against these evils. I was the lucky one because we shared each others' interests: my children helped me and by discussing many topics, I knew what was happening in their lives. They had no time to be distracted : they left school and entered the Lyceum.

I made sure that I talked to Kairat as well. He was often late coming home and and I have to admit that I took this hard but I tried to meet my husband with a smile and have the table set for dinner. Before and after the accident I always gave him my full support, taking an interest in what was going at his workplace. We talked about everything under the sun with just one exception: jealousy. Whenever he was late, my imagination ran wild and I would grow depressed but if I questioned him, he would simply respond by saying: " Marzia, if I stayed at home with you all day who would provide for our family?" Being a very emotional person , my feelings would often overwhelm me, reducing me to tears as I wondered where he was and with whom, but in truth, I always trusted him.

Kairat and I have lived together for thirty seven years, twenty of which I have been confined to a wheelchair but he still worships me. "How have you managed to keep your relationship alive?!" asked my husband's friends' wives. A good wife can make a real man out of loser but a bad wife can diminish even the boldest of men. The secret is very simple : I have always been happy to share my joy in my husband's achievements with my children, grandchildren and friends and secure in the knowledge that I wholly support his work, he in turn, has taken every opportunity to advance his career. Of course, life does not always run smoothly and when troubles arise, we often give in to our feelings and emotions. We had arguments like everyone else but being so closely involved in each other's lives, we managed to succeed in maintaining a mutual understanding and love for one another and I made sure that I never revealed any of his deficiences to my relatives.

He didn't accompany me to Seoul for my fourth session of chemotherapy.Instead, he travelled to England to present his book *Under the Wolf's Nest: A Turkic Rhapsody*, to the Royal Geographical Society. He returned around the 15th or 16th of December, just before the celebration of Independence Day and his own birthday. I didn't feel very well after the course of chemotherapy but my mood was good: I could emphasise with both Kairat's success and his passion for history and when a keen interest in his work on Turkic history arose in Europe and he was invited to present a lecture in Cambridge, I was very proud of both my husband and our country. I didn't want to just stay at home during those four days of the holiday, especially since Kairat had just returned from his triumphant book presentation, so I decided to organise a party for the 17th. I made reservations at a restaurant and invited all of his friends. After the meal, we listened to a report by Khabar on the book's presentation in London. I had intended to go along for about an hour but ended up staying the whole evening. Wearing a wig to conceal my hair loss, I wanted our friends to see me as I once was: cheerful and vivacious.

Unfortunately our happiness was short-lived: The very next morning, we received news of my mother's death . She had died unexpectedly as a result of a pulmonary edema. I had hoped that she would be able to see spring and summer: ill health had rendered her bedbound but her heart was strong and she had a good appetite. I would have felt more comforted if she had departed from this world surrounded by relatives but since this had not been the case, my loss felt even more acute. She had been a devoted mother and her love for her children had been boundless. Despite being very ill after chemotherapy, and my family's protests concerning my diminished immunity to infection, I was determined to attend the funeral.I tried my best to avoid any direct contact with anyone but nevertheless, caught an infection...

TURN YOUR FACE FROM THE WALL, TAKE A DEEP BREATH AND GET READY TO FIGHT!

If your legs are paralysed, all of your organs become impaired. Our bodies are constructed in such a way that you have to move in order for all of the organs to function properly. In the case of people with spinal injuries, this necessitates physiotherapy and intervention which although painful are vital in the prevention of long -term organ malfunction.

Whilst I was I in hospital with a fracture I was advised by doctors that because I was in danger of contracting bedsores, my body had to be turned every three hours. It is difficult to describe one's instinctive fear of this procedure : I worried that any movement would cause further fracture or displacement which would cause me more pain. Being in hospital, you feel a little more confident by the fact that painkillers are so readily available but even still, you still feel terrified.

There are special techniques which must be applied when turning a body to prevent further damage to the spine. Generally these involve three people; one to support your hips, a second to support your shouldres and a third to support your legs. On the command of "one, two, three" everyone simultaneuosly lifts and turns your body. It was my responsibility to call to be turned every three hours and to have ignored this, would have proved life-threatening. When I was discharged from hospital, my bed was taken by a woman who had suffered similar fractures. She was accountant from Samsonovka village. On one of my visits as an outpatient to the neurosurgery department several months later, I was saddened to learn that this woman, Mariya, had died as a result of bedsores. Unable to overcome her fear of the procedure, she had refused to have her body turned...

Going to the toilet and the associated intimate procedures proved the hardest moments of my life as a disabled woman. The paralysation of my lower body meant that I suffered from urinary incontinence. Gone are the sensations felt by a normal healthy body and everything becomes spontaneous and out of your control, leaving you feeling bitter and ashamed. I was offered neither any literature nor advice from doctors to explain or counter this problem which made life particularly difficult and frustrating.

It was therefore up to me to find a solution. For the first five or six years, in order to improve the innervation I focused on working on my bladder's tonicity. I dreamt that one day the muscles of this organ would be restored but up until now this deficiency is still present. I can only say that this process is under my control: as a result of physiotherapy and exercise, from time to time, I experience the need to pee. But if I missed or didn't pay immediate attention to this sensation, my body would not wait and I felt uncomfortable when my husband and my children became unwitting accomplices of my shame.

I became truly aware of the real problems connected with the residual urine when I came home from hospital! My trained bladder's tonus was far from adequate and since it could not discharge all of the liquid , there was always a residue of 250 to 400 grams of urine.

Nowadays I am a patient of Lyudmila Aleksandrovna Redko at the clinic commonly known as that of the Council of Ministers.

It is my hope that here, my kidneys and bladder can be restored to function properly. My nephrologist takes her patients' problems seriously and is a friendly and excellent communicator: I believe that it is due to the efforts of this doctor that I am still alive and had I not met her, I would never have been able to either travel the world or build houses.

When I was receiving treatment for my kidneys, several of the doctors doing their rounds would try to persuade me to accept a cystoma; a kind of catheter which directly discharges the urine from the bladder by means of a tube connected to an external bag. I rejected their advice completely. Oddly, I didn't feel like a disabled person despite being confined to a wheelchair, but I knew that if I had cystoma, my life would feel pointless. And I did succeed in overcoming my urinary problem and learned how to remove all of the residual liquid myself. Experts found it hard to believe but were soon convinced when their checks revealed that there was never more than a tablespoon of liquid left in my bladder. I would like to thank Ludmila Aleksandrovna.

In summer 2001 I broke my leg and was unable to remove the residual urine. I went to Korea for consultation with a urologist-nephrologist, fearing that this problem would result in back discharge , when liquid by passes the ureter and goes directly to the kidneys. If I contracted a serious toxic infection, my kidneys would arrest, with a potentially fatal outcome. Fortunately, a medical examination employing specialist equipment proved that this was not the case.

My problems with defecation began when I was in intensive care. They tried in vain to clysterize me when I was unconscious and when I was transferred to the ordinary ward I was given an enema. Eighteen days later my the bowels were still blocked. They too had become paralyzed and while they remained motionless, it was impossible for water from the enema to reach them and it simply poured straight out. After fourteen failed attempts with enemas, Kairat's aunts, Dr Raufa-apay and Dr Sonya-apay, decided to use massage to open my bowels.

Afterwards , nurse Raisa Aleksadrovna (I shall remember forever, the names of all those who helped me) advised me that when preparing people with such prblems for surgery, bisacodyl suppositories are used to facilitate the purgation.

Eventually, it was determined that we would try to facilitate bowel movement every two days since it was difficult to do on a daily basis but if left for three days or more, toxins would reach a potentially dangerous level. I follow this schedule to this day and all of my relatives know that if Marziya has a toilet day she won't go anywhere until her bowels are empty. This is a golden rule which I follow to the letter. Every evening I also take purgative herbs and in the mornings, I use suppositories and do some exercises. However, the most effective help was provided by a folk healer.

When we moved to Almaty our university friends were so shocked by my state of health that they were anxious to help in any way possible. One day they arrived at our country cottage accompanied by Kajimkan-aga, a sixth Dan master and yoga specialist. My first question to him was not about recovering the use of my legs, but rather, how to manage my toilet problems. Now I follow a set of routine procedures but during that first year, despite exercising to the point of exhaustion from early morning till late evening, my bowles remained blocked. Kajimgan-aka taught me some yoga exercises which proved so successful that even on "toilet days", I was able to be on site at my building projects no later than 11am. This was a real achievement, given my physical condition.

When my toilet day is going well, everybody is releived but when things are difficult, I become silent and this affects the mood of those around me. I am not complaining but no-one wants to watch me suffer, preferring to share my joy when I'm talking, laughing, cooking, serving up meals, teaching , telling stories or even scolding.

Why are toilets not communal areas? Because such intimate procedures as emptying one's bowels and bladder are performed in private. But if a disabled person requires an enema, they must have assistance and being deprived of your privacy is depressing and psychologically, very hard to bear .By overcoming my shame and discomfort, I am now able to talk about it and hope that my experience can help others who find themselves in a similar situation.

Finding a successful solution to this physiological problem increases the quality of life of a disabled person by as much as fifty per cent. Ways of adapting solutions depends on the condition of each individual patient. The spinal cord is unique; it can be damaged, broken and hurt in different places and it is therefore impossible to advocate any technique which would work for everyone.

One memorable event that had a serious impact on my life took place after I had been sent home. We were seeking different ways to facilitate my life. The doctors advised the use of a rubber bedpan whilst sitting upright since this makes it much easier to defecate. When you're lying down, your bowels are relaxed and switched to the "off" position. On this particular ocassion, I felt an urge but could not answer it immediately because I was awaiting the arrival of guests, some of the many who came to visit Kairat during this period. So Aselya and I went over to our neighbour Fatima's flat . She and her family had gone see to relatives in Kabardino-Balkaria and she had given me a key and asked me to look after the flat in her absence.

I had no problems with sitting over the bedpan but was worried about how I would then remove it as I only had my eleven year old daughter with me. I felt desperate and choked with tears just wanted the ground to open up.However, my darling girl who had become very upset by my distress yet far from embarrassed, cried out: ""Mummy, mummy! I can do it: I can make you clean. Please don't cry!"

AIDS FOR THE DISABLED ARE AS NECESSARY AS MATHEMATICS IN REACHING A LOGICAL SOLUTION

Kairat Zakiryanov

To become an integral part of society and not be condemned to a lonely and painful existence, disabled people require three things.

First, they must learn to relieve themselves without any assistance. Second, they must be guaranteed practical, moral and financial support. It is good that Marziya is supported by me and her children but I am not sure that the person who we love so much could have coped with her condition had she lived alone...

And thirdly, from a wider perspective, the needs of the disabled must be recognised and sensitively addressed, then financed, by society. In 1996,while working in the President's Administrative office, I arranged for the first time in the history of independent Kazakhstan, a meeting between disabled people and the President. Amongst those present was Alexander Vagner , a disabled man who had crossed Balkhash and organised a march from Moscow through all of the republics of the CIS. In honour of this deed he had received an award for courage which was presented by the President of the Russian Federation, Boris Yeltsin. I knew him well and Sasha often came to visit us in our country cottage. Unfortunately he has now departed this world: He had problems communicating with his family and made the decision to take his own life.

If disabled people are to have any chance of engaging in activities in the public sphere or simply being included in society, attention must be paid to making public tranport fully accessible. Despite the fact that abroad, taxis and buses have been specially adapted to provide ramps and elevators for wheelchairs, it remains almost impossible in our country to find one taxi which would enable a disabled person to travel independently, and until very recently, there was so little regard for the disabled that even incontinence pads were in short supply.

Marziya had a friend who was also confined to a wheelchair but she died as a result of her pension being so meagre that she could not afford taxis to take her to hospital. It's a sad truth that in order to afford the necessities of life, you need a reasonable income. Thankfully I am able to support my wife but what about the other half a million disabled people living in Kazakstan?

In mathematics, logic is used to define and then solve a problem. If the same were to be applied to the needs of the disabled, they would not only play a more active role in society but could also realise their own goals on either a domestic or professional level. In addition to obvious aids such as ramps, it is equally important that support groups are established and funded to ensure that the disabled enjoy a social life and do not become cut off or indeed, hidden, from society. My wife managed to immerse herself in society through her building projects but she also has her family and a wide circle of devoted friends, including Fatima who has benefited from Marziya's moral support ever since she too found herself confined to a wheelchair.

Life can't stop when you hear that your wife will no longer be able to walk and I have done everything in my power to ensure that she leads a balanced life. When my wife goes to Seoul for treatment, I hire a nurse to take care of her and make sure that someone is available to carry her wheelchair onto the plane. This allows Marziya to turn the focus of her attention away from her disability. I also hired Stanislav Savelyev , a specialist trainer, to make adaptions to things around the house and we even ordered artificial limbs to help her move around.

Finally, arrangements were made for Marziya to attend a clinic in Germany.The proposed course of treatment was due to run for sixty days, but after examining her medical report, the doctors advised that they would be give us a refund since they would be unable to improve her condition. Marziya accepted their decision but still insisted that they at least helped her find ways of adapting to everyday life.

All of our houses , designed and constructed under her guidance, were provided the ramps so that each was easily accessible from street level. Similarly, attention was paid to making the bathrooms and toilets as spacious as possible. The house in which my son and his family live, also has an elevator.

GET BETTER SOON : WE MISS YOU

Many people who find themselves in a similar position to mine, become rancourous and I met quite a few of these characters during the early years of my disability while we were living in Ust-Kamenogorsk. One of them confided to me that he wanted to pick up a gun and shoot anyone who could walk. He was very embittered. I am the kind of person who would ordinarily do anything I could to help someone like this to rise above such despair but faced with my own physical problems, I turned a deaf ear and seeing my former world destroyed, could only ask myself what I had left to live for.

Family and friends, in an attempt to raise my hopes, brought me various literary reports on my type of condition. I just couldn't conceive the extent of my disability. I was convinced that within a short time I would be able to get up and walk especially after reading an incredible article which described how a well-known weight-lifter, Valentin Dikul, had managed to overcome his paralysis through self-help.

After being in intensive care , I was moved to an ordinary ward and unaware of the severity of my condition, I unexpectedly advised my husband that one's own attitude of mind can prevail over the opinions of medics. I was discharged from the hospital with bedsores on the sacrum but since my mother and sisters had no specialist knowledge, they were unable to treat them. I was therefore lucky to find help from one incredible woman : Zagila, wife of Rashid Jakupov and Kairat's second cousin Zagila, worked at the maternity hospital close to our house and immediately offered to help even though we hardly knew each other. No matter how severe the weather, (in Ust-Kamenogorsk the temperature can drop to -45 degrees in winter with ferocious snowstorms) she visited me every night to apply fresh dressings. Gradually, she only needed to come every two days but this continued for eight months, from October to May. In my opinion, her totally selfless assistance is a great testimony of her dedication to her medical profession. By the time I set off for Saki in spring 1992, my wounds had completely healed and today I want to say to Zagila: thank you for saving me and for being such fun. We changed from being doctor and patient to close friends. Do you remember the time when we went to the hill at Chechek near Ust Kamenogorsk, for New Year's Eve; dancing and breaking crystal glasses with hearts filled with joy?!

... Being so pragmatic , I have not lost my sense of adventure or romance. One day about five or six years ago, my friends were round and on the spur of the moment I announced "Come on girls, let's kick up our heels! Fifty is no age limit to having some fun!" It was quite late at night when I persuaded them to go to Chymbulak. Abay, my faithful assistant drove us by jeep to the summit where the surrounding mountains and stars seemed so close that we felt that we could reach out and touch them. We were three middle-aged women but enjoyed partying like young girls and having disturbed a majestic silence of mountains with the music of Vysotsky and Pugacheva, my favourite singers, we opened a bottle of wine and toasted them. We had enjoyed our moments of reckless fun so much that we all agreed to get together again soon but unfortunately I fell ill shortly afterwards and now my friends will need to wait until I am better to join them. "Stop being sick", they implore me, "We're missing you!"

The other person who had a serious impact on the first years of my illness was Stanislav Petrovich Savelyev, a masseur with a God-given talent, He started calling on me when I was in hospital and then came to see us skiing. He devoted a lot of time on me and every day, spent between one and three hours massaging pressure points in an attempt to awaken cells within my spinal cord. Nothing came of it but thanks to the clever fingers of Stanislav Petrovich the bedsores healed more quickly. I was not his only patient; day after day, he volunteered to massage the painful hands and legs of many old women. It was about five or six years ago that I first met him but since then, our relationship has ended. It is never easy for someone so devoted to helping others to continue to serve us all…

After being discharged, I underwent regular checks and was given a lot of medication. In December more than four months after my fracture, I began to take an interest in what the doctors had prescribed and believed that both the medicines and injections were part of my treatment. However, it soon transpired that they were simply being employed as pain relief.

I had argued that I did not want to depend on painkillers for the rest of my life but when I refused to take them, I was in so much pain that I was unable to sleep. Happily at that time, the "Santa Barbara" series was launched on TV and as I lay watching it, I prepared myself for sleep by recalling what had happened on the show as well as all the good times I had had before my accident.

And I found great solace in nature, something which I had previously taken for granted. My most pleasant memories are connected to my country cottage in Ust Kamenogorsk. Whenever I felt weary, I would sit on a grassy knoll and look out at the magnificent view towards the forest, hills and river stretching into the distance.

And now between courses of chemotherapy I find refuge in my much loved garden. When I feel especially bad after treatments in Seoul, Kairat takes me for a walk around our garden. I like flowers and trees. A special place in my garden is dedicated to magnolias: there is one named after my granddaughter, Tomiris, and another named Tamerlan, in honour of my eldest grandson. The "Genghis Khan" magnolia was planted after Kairat had been elected as a Member of the World Academy of Genghis Khan in Mongolia. We spent our money wisely when we bought that magnolia which we named after the great military leader.

Over the last two years I have enjoyed seeing my favourite varieties of tulips bloom each springtime and my garden blossom further. I am always fascinated by this annual process which makes me all the more aware of how quickly my grandsons are growing up. At the same time, the anticipation of spring has always helped me to look ahead. It's a pity that I am no longer able to tend my garden myself. These days, Lera Herzen the gardener, and Nurkanat Akedilov my assistant, help me look after it.

When I first became disabled, I feared that my world would be confined to a hospital ward but once I had my wheelchair I realised that I could travel the world. Kairat and I, along with our grandchildren, have visited the Canary Islands, Bali, Turkey, Cyprus, Egypt, China, and the Arab Emirates; we've been to Hong Kong, Singapore, Paris, Prague, Rome, Venice, Istanbul and Moscow …

Later I took up smoking. This was connected not only to my pain but also, to my physiological state and problems defecating. One of my friends, who smokes, told me that for some reason, she could not go to the toilet until she had smoked a cigarette and suggested that I give it a try. I had smoked as a student, but it was a passing fad and when I fell ill I simply forgot about it. Now, when I tried smoking in my new condition I found that it did indeed, help to alleviate the problem. At the beginning

I was smoking every two days, and then I decided to give up. I had been abstaining for three days and… I couldn't stand it! I was wounded by the idea that I had allowed myself to fall prey to an addiction to nicotene especially since it took me almost a year to kick the habit. Ironically, this was largely due to two incidents which had little to do with willpower! I was living on a pension and suddenly found that I could no longer afford to buy cigarettes when yet another economic crisis sent the price soaring. And then, my son forgot to buy me the cigarettes which I had asked him to bring via a message on his pager. Three days later my husband and daughter noticed that I stopped smoking and I decided that fate had intervened to make me quit once and for all.

I didn't try to get into the wheelchair until after the New Year. After the failed operation, I had developed an animal-like fear that if I made any movement, I would break something else and for this reason, I initially wore a corset whenever I used the wheelchair.

When I entered the kitchen in my wheelchair for the first time to join my family for tea, my mother exclaimed with delight "Now you're really back in the world of the living!"

That day is also memorable because I washed my plate myself. It was not easy. Being on my back for so long had left its mark. I had received massage but my hands lacked coordination. I was hardly able to reach the tap and did not have the force of strength to turn it. I was dripping with sweat…but I did it!

I WILL BE THERE FOR YOU

Kairat Zakiryanov

There was never any doubt in my mind, regardless of the situation and the fact that Marziya was now paralysed, that I would ever remarry. Being a pragmatic person I was thinking not only of myself but also, our children. If it had not been for her, who knows what might have become of Baurzhan. Many of my son's friends ended up in prison and some of them became drug addicts. He was only able to cope with all of this through his mother's trust and the fact that she spent a long time talking to him.

Many of my own plans and ambitions were shelved as soon as my wife suffered her misfortune but my prime concern was to look after my darling whose life was so closely intertwined with mine.

My attitude is far removed from that of the traditional nomad, who for centuries, always placed the welfare of blood relatives high above that of his wives, since unlike parents or brothers, a wife could be easily replaced. As I anxiously hung about the hospital trying to recover from the shock of what had happened, I realised that it would now be up to me to provide enough money to support my family since my wife would no longer be able to work. My first priority was to raise fifty thousand dollars to send my wife for treatment in Germany and here, I would like to express my gratitude to Bagdat Shayakhmetov, my friend and President of the Ust-Kamenogorsk Titan-Magnesium Plant, for helping my family not only during the early years following the accident but also, more recently, when we found ourselves in dire straits.

The continuation of my close relationship with my wife after the accident undoubtedly appeared strange to many people. I was still young, only thirty six years old, and was surrounded by beautiful women. Focusing on my profession, I was quickly ascending my career ladder, moving from Deputy Rector to Rector and then to a post in the President's Administration Office before becoming and Rector of Higher Education at the Almaty Institute. My desertion of my family would have been deemed by some as perfectly normal since after all, how far could a successful man go when saddled with a disabled wife?

It is Lubov Polishuk who said that true love is the union of minds, hearts and bodies but if one of these is absent, love cannot survive. Marziya was not the same as before but my love for her remained as strong as ever, in every respect. She is my wife first and foremost, then my friend, the mother of my children, the grandmother of my beloved grandchildren and my partner in all of my business enterprises.

I don't know what fate has in store but it is my wish that we shall continue sharing our lives together well into old age.

When people say that men can only love healthy and beautiful women, this is also true. I fell in love with her because of her brightness and beauty. Then, when we became friends I appreciated from the perspective of a simple man brought up in the countryside, how well she organised our everyday lives. I told her: "I want to be with you forever; I can't imagine finding a more perfect wife." With these few words I declared the love I felt for her with my heart and soul. There are many occasions when a man falls in love with a beautiful girl, marries her and within one month parts from her because she lacks the qualities proper to a wife and prospective mother of his children. As Mayakovskiy said: "There is no going back if love is lost as result of a lack of harmony in daily life"

THE SLOW JOURNEY TOWARDS ACHIEVING OUR GOALS

On May 1992 we travelled to Crimea for specialist treatment in Saki city. It was here that I was strongly advised to remove the corset so that my muscles could start working for themselves. Initially, this resulted in my being unable to stay upright and my body swayed from side to side. After a while, when we were living in Ust-Kamenogorsk, I began to rise at six and whilst my family was still asleep, taught myself, step by step, how to dress, wash and make breakfast for myself before getting on with the administration of new construction projects. It was important to me that I was able to undertake each of these tasks by myself since I didn't want to be a burden to my children.

There are special techniques which can enable disabled people to turn themselves over and move from their beds to their wheelchairs unassisted but in the beginning, without instruction, I had to master these manoeuvres by trial and error and was still dependent on help from my ten year old daughter, Asel. My son, Baurzhan who was only fifteen at the time, carried me to the bathroom.

While Baurzhan was charged with the hardest housework, Asel washed and ironed her father's shirts and both learned how to become expert cooks. Some may think that these responsibilities were too much for children but it was simply the case that neither wanted an outsider, someone employed as a domestic help, living in our house.

Later on, after I had been taught the correct procedures at the clinic in Bayreuth, Germany, I became far more independent.

My children had to grow up quickly. When my daughter entered her first year at high school, we were living in the KShT micro-district, one of the most densely populated in the city. Her school which was located across the road from our house had as many as eleven first year forms with forty children in each class. Aselya was one of the best pupils but I soon began to notice that my daughter was not being challenged. I told my husband that my children's education was more important than them having to look after me. At first, Kairat didn't agree with me, saying that our daughter should continue coming home at break times to help me but I eventually won the argument and in the second term, Aselya was transferred to the best Lyceum in Ust Kamenogorsk. She usually travelled by herself, changing from one bus to another but from time to time, we took advantage of one of the privileges attached to Kairat's position and she was picked up by her father's driver in the company car.

At her previous school my daughter had always excelled and I was afraid that the stricter regime of the Lyceum would diminish her confidence and cause her to lose her hunger for learning. I therefore tried to prepare her by advising: "Your grades will be average at first but don't get upset! You'll soon see how quickly you'll catch up and then you'll be top of the class again. I'll be here to help you».

I was right. She had to work hard to master one of the subjects not taught at her last school but by the end of the year my daughter was once again one of the top pupils.

Baurzhan and Aselya gave meaning to my life. From the day they were born, I felt bound to educate them and lick them into shape. After a while they became used to the fact that I was confined to a wheelchair .When Kairat worked late, Asela was always with me. During our long evenings together she recalled: "Mum, remember when you used to look out of our bedroom window and call down 'Children! Aselya! Baurzhan! It's dinner time. Wash your hands!' We would come running in and be served an array of delicious dishes." Hearing this I burst into tears. My girl who until recently, had not been allowed to handle a knife, was now the one who had to cook and look after her mum.

It gave me the impetus to restore this aspect of my previous life and slowly, I was once again able to prepare the children's lunch for when they came in from school. To achieve this, I imagined myself in my children's and Kairat's shoes and was determined from then on to not only anticipate, but eliminate, all negative aspects of my part in their lives.

A DESIRE TO DANCE

One day Kairat called me and told me to get ready for a banquet at the region's Akim's Residence. The banquet had been arranged in honour of Erejep Alkhairovich Mambetkaziyev who for the first time after becoming Minister of Education, was coming to Ust Kamenogorsk.

The initial reaction was not to go! This was not only due to the fact that I would need to get ready by myself (I now go to the beauty salon for manicures and hairdressing) but because I felt embarassed about appearing in public. Moreover, it was hard for me to remain in a sitting position for any length of time since it hurt my back. It was a high society event which would have been a challenge for any wife of a newly appointed Rector. But Kairat insisted and I had to obey. When I arrived everyone had assembled inside but the doorstep was so high that I was unable to ascend in my wheelchair and had to be carried in. As I entered, everyone arose and ministers, akims and their wives all rushed to greet me and congratulate me on my husband's promotion.

At the time, I didn't ask Kairat why it had been so important that I attend this event but fairly recently I felt compelled to find out, especially since it had required such great effort. My question angered him so much that he refused to answer but knowing that I would persist, he finally replied: «It was not only a moment of triumph for the Minister but for me too, as his successor. I wanted you, as my nearest and dearest to be at my side since you have supported me all the way through. I also wanted you there because by attending receptions, parties and dances you will become as much a part of this world as an able-bodied person».

Since then, we have attended every important event together, regardless of how I'm feeling. That included occasions when there were disputes concerning the Academy of Sport during which my husband's opponents did everything in their power to undermine Kairat in the mass media. This included hurtful rumours about my husband's love affairs which I had to bear through gritted teeth . I tried to follow him wherever he went and despite sometimes being the focus of many people's adverse attention, I just smiled and looked with eyes full of love at my husband.

We are never bored with each other and even in moments of silence, feel very close to one another. Although my children often comment that their mother has the last word, no-one is the dominant partner in this relationship. It is normal when we are "at war" that each retreats into their own world for a while, waiting to see who will be the first to relent. As a rule it is Kairat who steps forward to make the peace: "Even though I'm not guilty, I'm sorry anyway." And I'll return to the subject of the argument by exclaiming: "What made you behave like that?!" I must always make sure that he takes back his words.

… There is no harm in dreaming. If one day a miracle occurred and I became like I used to be, the first thing I would like to do is dance with Kairat. When we were young we never missed a dancing-party at the University or in the Halls. However before going anywhere we promised each other not to dance with anybody else.

My favourite dance is the waltz although many people make so many mistakes and are so clumsy that they can appear to be messing around with this noble dance! But I loved it so much! Nowadays if I'm feeling good, I dance at parties by using my hands, shoulders and hips to turn my wheels forwards and backwards. It's not proper dancing but my friends like to see me joining in.

HAVE WHEELCHAIR, WILL TRAVEL

When we moved to Almaty, it became routine practice to attend official parties arranged by local akims (I have very pleasant memories of Viktor Vyacheslovovich Khrapunov who invited me to all his New Year parties). Wherever I went I was always greeted with respect but I do hope that this was not due to my disability. I was really glad to receive an invitation from Astana's akim, Imangali Nurgalievich Tasmagambetov to take part in the capital's 15th Anniversary celebrations. Naturally I could not have refused, especially since we had been provided with an official car and I had the opportunity to tour the new Astana . Imangali Nurgalievich considered me to his close friend and whenever we found ourselves at the same function, he always came forward to greet me.

Trips are a large part of my life with Kairat. The first long trip after the accident was to Crimea, to Saky city. I recall the time when even thinking about boarding a plane made me scared. But even though this was more than twenty years ago, the airport provided good facilities for disabled passengers, with special medical services that made it possible to carry a disabled person into the cabin either physically or by means of an adapted wheelchair. On arrival at the destination, the airport again offered assistance with transferring the disabled passenger into his or her own wheelchair where they feel far more comfortable.

The first years are very hard for any disabled person who has decided to immure themself. You have not yet mastered how to manouevre yourself from wheelchair to car and you need to be lifted. Then you must become skilled in manipulating the disabled person's board to facilitate moving from one seat to another. Many disabled drivers are able to operate their folding wheelchair independently: they get into the driver's seat and move their wheelchair to the passenger seat.

I'm relating these facts by way of encouraging disabled people who feel anxious about travelling. There are just as many disabled people today as there were twenty years ago but many are still reduced to begging in order to survive. Attitudes towards disability are however, changing little by little. Public buildings now have ramps, not always ideal but there nevertheless. Those which don't and where the provision of external elevators is impossible, still makes it necessary for assistance to be given to wheelchair users, often involving severe jerking movements of the chair up steps and causing discomfort and the risk of the person being tipped out. Some wheelchair users are able to manage this themselves but only if the steps are not too narrow or slippery and their arms are strong enough.

Essentially, the ease with which a wheelchair user can travel around still depends very much on the willingness of other people and particularly, passers-by, to offer assistance when needed, and the availability of such help rests very much on people's attitudes ,courtesy and care towards others. The first year after my accident I devised a project to establish a residential treatment centre; I wanted to be involved in public activities and to draw the attention of the authorities to people with problems similar to mine. In retrospect, I should have realised immediately that my domestic situation could not accommodate a fully- fledged campaign and instead, I should have confined myself to raising a petition for changes and improvements for the care of the disabled. I have two teenage children and am without either assistants or a car. I had no right to distract my children by loading them with my troubles. Their lives were already very busy: in addition to looking after me they had school, courses and housework and there was simply no time for them to increase their duties if their mother became involved in public campaigns. I therefore decided to abandon such projects.

My life was dedicated to my children and their education and I worked hard at maintaining a close sense of family as well as my own self esteem.

I was equal to this task and it was perhaps easier for me to maintain a spiritual bond with my children than other mothers, since my condition meant that by necessity, I spent a great deal of time at home with my children and was able to talk to them as they undertook housework and when my daughter was helping me dress or my son was assisting my movement around the house.

Similarly, in contrast with their peers who were beginning to lead more independent lives, my children were in the home when their father returned from work and so were involved in conversations about his day too. The close bond which evolved during those years continues to this day despite our now being physically separated.

IT TAKES EFFORT!

After the accident and as a result of stomach problems, I lost my appetite and my sister suggested a change of diet, including the introduction of green cucumber smeared with black caviar. In despair, she continually asked me what I would like to eat and on demand, prepared my favourite dishes but I still had no appetite and grew depressed by the terrible thought that I would never again find any pleasure in food.

Once my stomach problems had cleared up, concentrated efforts were made to restore the normal functioning of my intestines and I was placed on a high fibre diet comprising a variety of fruit and vegetables, especially oyster mushrooms, alongside a smaller quantity of glutinous food. At the time I had not yet contracted diabetes and was able to eat whatever I wanted without gaining excess weight. However, in common with many women going through the menopause I realised that not only was I more susceptible to putting on weight but shedding those extra kilos was not as simple as it used to be!

And what can I tell you about procedures for washing and bathing? My Model 400 wheelchair was provided with a water-resistant derma tin at the base for when I needed to freshen up. The showers in my apartment and later, my house had both been adapted so that I could wheel my chair in easily. I am still afraid, however, to get into the bath by myself and so relied on assistance from my relatives.

Surfing the internet can provide numerous techniques to help the disabled fend for themselves but research takes time. I would have far preferred someone to provide demonstrations but unfortunately, didn't know anyone with similar problems to mine. It was therefore quite difficult to anticipate all of the nuances of my situation. Moving onto one particular bed would present one challenge but since each chair and bed tended to be a different height, I had to concentrate hard and adapt my movements to avoid causing further injury or physical damage. Obviuosly, until I had fully mastered these techniques, someone had to be present in case I fell. When I was in Germany, I was advised that the bones of paralysed people are inclined to lose calcium, making them more fragile. To counteract this, your diet must contain calcium-rich dairy foods, especially cheese. I was also told to avoid placing any pressure on my legs, such as leaning on them, since now that they were more brittle, the bones would be prone to fracture. Their position was also important and I learnt how to move them with my arms to prevent them from twisting.

So how did I ever manage to leave the house? When I went for treatment in Germany in 1995 I was given a very thin, yet solid board. One end was placed under your bottom in the wheelchair and the other end was placed on the surface of whatever you wanted to sit on, a chair or a bed. You then had to slide yourself across the board by using your arms and by pulling your legs with your hands. This was one manoeuvre which definitely requires a demonstration by either another person. I have always been opposed to motorised wheelchairs because I am of the opinion that if you don't use your arms and hands, you aren't working any part of your body. That is why no matter tired I feel or how sore my hands, I always turn my wheels myself. Of course when I go to the countryside my friends, Kairat or the children are always with me, so can help me by pushing the chair along rough tracks. Similarly, when I am visiting building sites or travelling abroad, I have assistance.

I have lived my life true to my nature and my upbringing: I have always expressed an utmost respect for my country, teachers and war veteran father, and have always been highly motivated, bearing a strength of character which has helped me overcome most obstacles. My decision to refuse to take painkillers was based on the logical conclusion that over time, they would affect my liver and cause more serious problems with my health. Similarly, I rejected sleeping pills since they adversely affected the function of my intestines and nervous system, and Validol was dismissed because it overly relaxed all of my muscles, including again, those of my intestines which would have resulted in an accumulation of waste in these and other organs.

BECOMING AN INDEPENDENT WOMAN

For five or six years after the accident I had been desperately fighting to restore the innervation of my spinal cord: I ran myself into the ground while getting about on crutches and on Dikul's apparatus, I cycled as well. Meantime Kairat had been visiting many business enterprises in Ust Kamenogorsk in search of funding for my treatment abroad. In 1995 we finally managed to raise the required sum and I went for two months' treatment in Bayreuth, Germany.

The Head physician at the clinic for disabled people with similar problems to mine spent forty five minutes talking to me. When I mentioned to my physiotherapist that I had felt uncomfortable about the professor spending so much time on me, Anita began to laugh: "If he had no interest in talking to you, you would have found yourself outside. He even told me that he hadn't expected to have such a meaningful conversation with you!"

But to be honest, I had been preparing for this consultation for some time and I had questions that I had been unable to find answers for in Kazakhstan. I wanted to know, for example, if it were possible to prevent stagnation in a paralyzed person's body. As far as possible, each cell of our body must be able to move in order for all of the organs to function normally, otherwise waste products accumulate.

The answer was physiotherapy and exercising in a pool but this was very difficult to organise during the 1990's in a small provincial town. Nowadays, it is still not easy to access such treatment but with the support of friends and relatives, access can be gained to the relevant facilities. If a disabled person has no-one to accompany them to such facilities, help can be sought from charitable organisations, various associations and social media networks designed to provide you with both friends and helpers.

I haven't been to the pool for the past two years because of my bedsores but before the accident, I swam like a fish. When I became paralysed I felt that my life had ended with regard to my dream of seeing the world and swimming in different seas and oceans but today, I get a little confused about the number of countries I've visited with Kairat! Each year we go to Issyk-Kul and we've also travelled to Karlovy Vary, Turkey, the Emirates, Malaysia, Thailand, Taiwan, Singapore, Seoul, China, Bali, Hong Kong and the Canary Islands. One day on holiday in Cyprus, we bet who could hold their breath underwater for the longest. I managed to stay under for two and a half minutes, much to the alarm of some foreigners who came over to check that I was still alive!

It's worth relating how I swam for the first time after becoming paralysed. When we were still living in Ust-Kamenogorsk, Kairat asked me to accompany him on a visit to the Bukhtarmin reservoir. It had been our intention to go boating but when we were having a picnic on the bank,

I decided that I wanted to go for a swim and so was fitted with a lifejacket and carried into the water. I began to swim using the breaststroke but noticed that no matter how intensive my strokes, I remained in the same position. In utter despair, I cried " I can't do it!" and then heard Kairat respond " I can't either!" It transpired that fearing that I would drown; he had been holding onto my legs! When he released me, I managed to reach the jetty and asked for my lifejacket to be removed since I felt that it restricted my movement.

Later I learned how to dive directly into the pool from my wheelchair , much to the surprise of everyone around me. Many people with a similar disability to mine (generally foreigners) feel quite comfortable in the water and even manage to get out of the pool unaided.

The first house I built only had a bath which was hardly used on account of how long it took to get me in and out of it. However, the new house in which Kairat and I are now living, has a small pool equipped with the ramp so I can swim even when home alone.

PITY CAN ONLY LEAD TO A DEAD END

Everywhere in the world there are people who are willing to take on board other people's problems: you only need to find them. But if you are of an unhappy disposition, constantly complaining about your lot, then it is unlikely that anyone or anything will ever meet your expectations for a better life and you will be left with nothing.

Not long ago, there was a report on Malakhov's programme entitled: "Let them speak". It concerned a woman who came across a fourteen year old Russian boy who had suffered an accident in Turkey and had lost his memory. The woman had her own problems: she was divorced, had no permanent abode and had three children and yet she was determined to take care of this child, with the support of her ex-husband and sons.

From the outset, I tried to do everything by myself, something which earned me the respect of everyone around me, especially my children and husband. In Germany I was even nicknamed "Mrs Independent"! Whenever the nurse charged with looking after me, rushed to assist me, I always replied: "No, I'll do myself'" and she would have to stand back and watch whilst "Mrs Independent" would manoeuvre herself from bed to wheelchair and go to exercise classes or the swimming pool. Why did I act like this? Because I was afraid of losing the skills and techniques I'd mastered three years ago. If you're lucky, you will have the opportunity to attend a residential centre where you will be taught how to move your body by yourself. Otherwise, it's up to you to master these techniques.

My self-sufficiency was achieved at a high price since I am the kind of person who pushes themselves to the limit but I believe that this character trait allowed me to overcome my depression following the accident and enabled me to embark on a new life.

In Bayreuth I was still being kept awake by the same pains that I had experienced at home and as a distraction, would sit on the terrace reading books which I'd brought with me. It was springtime, the trees were in blossom and the birds sang. The two months spent in Germany left unforgettable impressions, not least because I never imagined that I would travel abroad.

I had travelled alone since Kairat had commitments at work. One day, my interpreter and escort who was a German language teacher in SUEK, blurted out: "Everybody knows about your situation and how tight your finances are." When you become older you come to realize that people love talking about situations where one of a married couple comes to grief and this can be very hurtful. People in my country are particularly guilty of this. When I went shopping I often overheard my countrywomen making comments about my physical disability. They thought that I couldn't understand what they were saying because they assumed that since I didn't look like a Kazakh, I didn't speak the language. I felt really upset when I heard them muttering "What's she doing here?" implying that anyone in a wheelchair had no right to mix with the able-bodied or block their path with a wheelchair! It didn't occur to them that they too could find themselves in the same predicament one day. I never encountered such prejudice when travelling abroad to Western countries and indeed, if anyone in Germany saw me struggling to get myself up steps, they would immediately rush to my aid.

In this country I acquired a lot of friends. The nurses took me shopping or to the parks and during the weekends when there weren't any treatments, my interpreter Rosa and Valera,her husband, would happily escort me around town. It was a revelation that I was allowed to go out for a walk, especially since I came across many other disabled people also being accompanied by their escorts. Psychologically, regardless of nationality whether German, Kazakh or Russian, all of us who are disabled would give anything for a complete cure. However, in countries like Germany, public awareness , access and financial support for the disabled are far more advanced and consequently, provide people like me with a welcome sense of security. Their mental attitude to disability is also quite different to ours. During that period, in 1995, if anyone in the family became disabled, a relative would be formally entitled to take care of them.

And what happens in our country? If you are disabled, you are required to provide evidence of how you reached that state and there is no guarantee of any help being provided. In contrast, the Germans' procedure is far more practical and supportive. I remember one German girl, Ani, who had broken her cervical vertebra when she jumped off a diving board. Every day this twelve year old, heavily corseted girl was visited by relatives: parents, grandparents and aunts. "Everything will be fine" they repeated over and over again. " We'll soon get her into a wheelchair." On days when she wasn't visited by relatives, the girl who was unnable to move either her arms or legs, was attended by a remedial gymnastics specialist, given massages and wiped down to prevent bedsores.

There are many cases which prove that recovery can be accelerated through encouragement from carers but sadly even now, the level of care offered to the disabled in my country falls far behind that provided in Germany in the mid- nineties.

Through contact with people whose disabilities resembled mine, in Saky and Beyreuth, I changed my mode of thinking and I realised that it is possible for anyone to retain an enthusiasm for life even when confined to a wheelchair. I am fully confident that any person, whatever their situation, can overcome self-pity and being pitied by others. Otherwise, you reach a dead end. People will naturally feel pity for you for a month, a year and perhaps a year more but after that, even your family will begin to feel the strain and consider you a burden if you expect pity or wallow in self-pity.

I repeat once again; I didn't want to be a burden to my children, my husband and my mother. This gave me the impetus to get moving; to wash and dress myself, to cook and clean and ultimately, to build houses.

I LIVE IN TWO PLACES:
MY HOME AND THE WORLD AT LARGE

Kairat Zakiryanov

I am proud of our President and our country's achievements. When I organised our International Conference at the Academy of Sports and Tourism, it was attended by over thirty Principals of universities specialising in physical education from all over the world. After the forum I invited our guests to visit Astana in order to show off our capital.

People will forget and have already forgotten that St. Petersburg was built on the bones, blood and suffering of many people. But does the same apply to Astana? Of course we cannot all live in penthouses, there will always be rich and poor people in every society.What do I mean by that ? The notion is very simple: people's rise to eminence is defined by their actions. All major decisions and events created on a national basis are not of course, comparable to Marziya's story, but any State consists of small cells, and the family unit is such a cell.

In addition to the large house which Marziya built for our son's family and which I believe will be our home for many years to come, she also constructed the small house in which we are currently living, as well as a Ski Centre for the Academy.

We started building our first house with a budget of only three thousand dollars, but it didn't scare her and when I reveal that the cost of the Sports stadium was only 500 dollars per square metre, no-one believes me. In Alma-Ata, the rate for a government funded building is over 1000 dollars per square metre but it should be noted that more than half of these funds are embezzled before it is ever completed.

Marziya worked within the limited resources entrusted to the Academy. She took personal charge of researching the market to find the cheapest prices for materials and went to Guangzhou in the south of China to buy equipment. She always sought quotes and was responsible for finding and employing labour at the best rates.

Some people may consider the family a more lowly cause but for Marziya, building the family was far more important than the construction of any building and we are indebted to her for our children's achievements: our son was awarded a PhD and was appointed Rector of the Academy of Sports and our daughter is a Candidate of Juridical Science and Associate Professor of the National University of Kyrgizstan. Now she dreams that her elder grandsons ,Tamerlan and Arslan, will study at Cambridge. And if they succeed , it will be due to their perspectives being widened by that person for whom they have utmost respect, their grandma.

GOD CONTINUES TO TEST ME

I built the Sports Stadium and completed the construction of the hotel with my assistant, Abay Akedilov. Vladimir Alekseevich Shestopalov, an employee of the Academy of Sports and a close colleague of Kairat , never tires of commenting: "Marziya, thank you for all you've done for Abay. He used to be so disorganized but you've managed to lick him into shape".

For my part, I consider it my duty to help young people who cross my path and to sort out their lives. Abay is very trustworthy, I think of him as my son and would be quite helpless without him.

In the early days when we went to my office and to save him from having to carry me all the way up to the fifth floor, I would ask "Abay, go up and have a look at the new quotes and then come down and tell me if they warrant our attention" At first he was hesitant and would exclaim, whilst grabbing my wheelchair: "Marziya-apay, let's go together" However, he quickly grasped a good understanding of the business and it was he who came up with the name of our sports stadium, *Kaymar*, based on the first syllables of my name and Kairat's.

The history of our construction company is an epic of sorts. Kairat had been trying to persuade me for two years to take on building contracts which other companies refused to touch. Despite bidding for these jobs, no contractors wanted the responsibility of working with such meagre budgets. Perhaps I too, would have shied away from such work, had Abay not insisted that he helped me. He was entrusted to manage the final stages of the construction of the hotel and also, the sports stadium. "Apay, I will do everything you tell me , you won't have to repeat anything twice. Let's do it!"

Kairat asked me to build the earthquake- resistant stadium on a turn-key basis, within a budget of 600 US dollars. And I did it; even though

I had to to fight for each kopek , I refused to disgrace myself by building anything which resembled a shed.

For the first two months of the contract, I gathered together quotes to find the most economical rates for materials and labour and was lucky to find a good builder in Ertay; a graduate in physical education from KazSU who proved himself highly responsible.

Construction was managed by me and Abay but since I had overall responsibility for the project, I ordered my assistant to photograph each stage for reference. Once the stadium had been completed, all of the photos, including those of the underground facilities, were exhibited in the gymnasium. According to calculations made by the Seismology Institute, the building would be able to withstand an earthquake reaching level ten on the Richter scale.

The construction of houses for the Zakiryanovs is an important aspect of my life. When Baurzhan and Asel got married I no longer felt needed. I grew depressed, lost weight and became sad to the point that when my daughter-in-law, Sveta called she anxiously asked "Are you okay, mum?"

My life felt as though it had lost its meaning and I explained to Kairat: "I gave birth to our son and daughter, and then because you were so busy, I brought them up practically by myself. I pointed them both in the right direction and now both of them are well educated, have good jobs and are married. I have also supported your career ever since you graduated. I never discouraged you from pursuing your own leisure interests, including visits to the bath house or hunting, even when I was ill. Now that all of your lives are complete and I have done my duty, I feel like I have no purpose. I can't just spend my life waiting for you to come home from work."

I was surprised by his response: "You're an amazing woman; it's true that you've devoted your life to us, the Zakiryanovs, but the one thing that you have yet to do is build us a house." His words cut me to the core and then I became exasperated. Waiting until I had calmed down, my husband reminded me when we had been allocated a plot of land by the akimat officials , we had neither ample funds nor the time to commence the build. Kairat was working full time and the children were studying and had their own lives to lead.

However, things had changed and my husband convinced me that instead of relying on Baurzhan to carry me down from the third floor every time I wanted to go outside, I should get on with making arrangements for the construction of our own little house. This conversation took place in October 2001 and in November I began working alongside other specialists on plans and then the build of our house. I was greatly inspired by the project and early each morning as soon as I woke up, I visited the site. I sourced all of the building materials myself : our budget was limited but wanting the best, I was prepared to barter for each and every nail and even made several visits to China where materials were less expensive. When we moved in, I was surprised and delighted by what I had achieved and decided to build a smaller house for just me and Kairat, using timber blocks which I managed to buy for a song in Katon-Karagay. Up until then, we had been living happily in the same house as Baurzhan and Sveta for eleven years but now that I was well able to manage the housework myself, it was time that they had a place of their own.

Shortly after we had moved into this small house, I was struck by bouts of illness, one after another. First, I broke my right leg whilst on holiday in Indonesia, and then an overdose of medication caused intoxication of my liver, followed by my contracting hepatitis, provoked by my diabetes.

When I felt better, we went on holiday to Turkey where I broke my left leg. It didn't heal properly and as a result, I suffered from pressure sores. In 2012 we decided to go to Seoul since we could access there, a much wider and more economical range of medication than anywhere in our own country. We also chose Seoul on the recommendation of Kajimkan Masimov, Jenya and Larisa An, friends who had helped take care of me when life had been especially hard for both me and Kairat. On my second day there, I was diagnosed as having reached the fourth and inoperable stage of my cancer.

MY HELPERS

As a rule, people who are ill can be very capricious. They often expect their assistants or nurses to work intuitively and when they awkwardly try to help, their patients become agitated and shout accusations that they're useless. The relationship between wheelchair-bound invalids and their assistants is worthy of psychological research. Anyone who is ill should learn to be patient and be prepared to relegate to the sideline, the pain and annoyance which emerge through poor communication. They should focus instead, on teaching their carers how to best deal with their needs. This applies to anyone in charge of looking after an invalid, whether they are paid or are doing so out of the goodness of their heart. People employed and paid to care for the sick have varying degrees of experience and their characters also impact upon their work. Some are naturally nurturing and are ready to listen to your needs but there are others whose attitude is indifferent, to say the least. They consider a nurse's job to be easy, restricted to administrating medicines and glasses of water but there is a lot more to it than that and those with the most altruistic characters undoubtedly make the best nurses. In my case, those carers who were able to meet my requirements and who continued working with me proved that they had survived and excelled in the school of hard knocks! In addition to providing me with medicines, their duties covered various elements of family life, including efficient housekeeping and cooking. I was probably particularly fussy about the cooking since, taught by my grandmother, I am an expert, able to produce in equal measure, simple tasty meals and more intricate, delicate dishes. I believe that my only granddaughter Tomiris also has a natural flair and she tells me that one day, she would like to become an restaurateur.

Other important qualities that I try to instil in my assistants are the foundations of spirituality and morality. I don't attempt to discuss subjects concerning good and evil with them but being older and a teacher by profession, I feel bound to impart knowledge stemming from what I have learned and experienced. In my opinion, any dialogue between people is mutually beneficial, regardless of their relationship, including that of an employer and employee. This helps to stabilise and strengthen relationships in many spheres, from business to family. As soon as this balance is disturbed, rows and treachery arise.

I have a good relationship with my assistant Abay and one which has developed from one of business colleagues to friendship. We have been working together for over ten years and he recently revealed that in all that time, he has never held a grudge against me despite my authoritarian character: "If you are not satisfied with my work it means that I missed something. I accept this without feeling opposed or displeased. In the early days, if you asked me to do something, I would automatically look for someone else to do it but time passed and I barely noticed how or when I began using my own initiative. I think I could now do anything you ask of me."

Abay came to me from Kizilorda as a very young man who tried to solve all his problems with his fists. Now he is highly respected and an economic manager. Whenever he picks up my phone calls he always asks: "Is everything okay?" He's used to me calling him on business matters and is afraid that one day I will be gone. Besides our friendship we share a common interest in our work. We've assisted each other in many projects and achieved harmony in our working relationship. It's not unreasonable that I should express my dissatisfaction, from time to time, and although he will sometimes deny that he is in the wrong, he will always come round when I explain the situation more clearly. I always try to avoid upsetting anyone without reason or purpose and no matter how important my role, I let the other person have the last word.

In fairness it must be said that before Abay, Kairat and I were helped by Abay's brother Jasnur or Jasik, as we called him. He travelled with me to China to buy building materials and accompanied us on holidays to Cyprus and Turkey. Now this baton has been passed to his younger brother: Nurkanat. According to his parents and friends he has changed a lot and has transformed from a reckless mamma's darling to a mature man and good manager. I do hope my efforts have played some part in this..

After living with us for a year, my husband's niece, Asem, came to me saying: "Aunt Marziy, you've given me a better insight to life in this one year than I've gained in all of my eighteen years. Thank you."

A MEETING THAT MIGHT NEVER HAVE HAPPENED

I return now to the early '90s when misfortune visited our house. I had refused to take painkillers and had forbidden my relatives to discuss the state of my health, since I wanted to spare them endless moaning. What could they do to relieve my pain? Absolutely nothing! They already felt helpless and if subjected to continuous moaning on my part, would undoubtedly have grown even more exhausted and frustrated, regardless of how much they loved me.

I found refuge in my favourite poems and Kairat still expresses his surprise that the first thing I asked for, having barely regained consciousness, was a volume of poems by Tyutchev!

Whenever I felt my body and soul harden, I also turned to the words of Izumrud Kulieva:

I won't become your habit,
Your ordinary working day.
I want to be everything that surrounds you
Personal and impersonal.

I want to be a holiday, spring,
Mute discovery, shock,
Transformation, revival,
Always the bride ,not your wife !

I will be the bright morning rainbow,
But not the page on the calendar.
Giving my thanks for every moment,
That you are young and joyful.

Music and poetry have helped me to overcome despair, depression and
pain. I particularly love Kazakh kui since for me, the dombra is a sacred
instrument.

It was with great pleasure therefore, that I attended a concert given by
Dmitry Khvorostovsky at the Congress Hall, during Astana's anniversary
celebrations. I particularly enjoyed a recital based on the words of my
favourite poet and it felt as though my own soul joined in that romantic
song:

I want to be your music,
The song that you haven't yet sung,
Your hidden torture,
Your bright dreams.
I want to be light leaves,
Your white snow,
Your shy kisses,
First and last.

I want to be both death and birth,
Your falling and recovery,
Your spring winds,
Willed and not willed.

I want to be the past that never comes back,
Your morning and evening,
Beloved and loved by halves,
Met and not met.

I want to be your win,
I want to be something that never comes true,
Your happiness (but not misfortune!),
Something that has happened, and is yet to come.

I want to be both death and birth,
Your falling and recovery,
Your spring winds,
Willed and not willed...

In autumn 2012, on 30 October, Kairat and I celebrated our 37th wedding anniversary and the date coincided with my first course of chemotherapy at the clinic in Seoul.

I've been asked many times how I've managed to maintain such a close bond with my husband. It was by chance that I ended up in Almaty and met Kairat. My grandfather had wanted me to study in Moscow but when my older brother left to continue his studies in the capital, he regularly sent me postcards from Almaty and I fell in love with this city before I'd ever been there.

I eventually visited the city, accompanying a classmate who had enrolled in the Talgara Medical College. Coming from the small town of Temir, Alamty felt like a foreign country and I spent a bewildering day wandering the city until I was advised to take a trolleybus direct to KazSU where I was to submit an application to study mathematics.

There was a delay in my being accepted for a place. My marks were borderline and although other students with similar points were admitted according to other criteria, the rest of us were told by Maruan Nadirkhanovich Sagitov, the Dean of the Faculty, that there was a possibility that we would be admitted only if and when, other students had been relocated to courses in Moscow, Novosibirsk and other large cities. I waited for two long weeks, regularly visiting the Dean's office, desperate to hear whether I had even a slender hope of being admitted to the faculty in Almaty. I was delighted when at last, the Dean congratulated each of us on gaining a place and I was able to send a telegram to my family with the good news.

All of us who had come from provincial towns were hard pushed to catch up on some of the subjects and we spent many days in the reading halls. I did however, manage to participate in sport and never missed any of the training sessions. In addition, I was appointed a member of the Komsomol's department and the Student's Council for Halls where we enjoyed vociferous debates on issues related to our public activities. I was put in charge of sanitation in the students' halls and as soon as I appeared in the corridor holding my notebook, some of the students would turn off their lights and close their doors! Naturally, my floor was the cleanest, in keeping with my aversion to dust in hidden corners! I was authorized to solicit the eviction of any students but being very strict I never used this power, preferring instead, to fight until my requirements were met.

Kairat had noticed me during matriculation, long before I was given any of these assignments, but he claims that he immediately fell in love with me when he came to apply for the room in the halls and spotted me crossing the corridor. For my part, I was oblivious to him and knew nothing about a certain Zakiryanow who had been accepted on the course.

We were studying in parallel groups but he shared a room with the male students from my group and I shared a room with girls from his group. Whenever he visited them to discuss course assignments, he always hoped that it would be me who would open the door.

In our Halls, there were students of biology, philosophy, economics, mechanics and mathematics. There were not enough places in the reading room for everyone so whilst the student on duty washed the floor and made supper, the girls from my room studied in our dormitory hall. When Kairat noticed me among them, he pulled his friend Vitaly Bloshitsyn aside and whispered: "Let's go along there so that I can see Marziya." At that time, I didn't take notice the look of love in his eyes.

During that first year, he held back and didn't declare his feelings for me and when I had my hair cut really short, he later admitted that he almost went off me!

When he did finally manage to pluck up the courage to approach me romantically, it was under strange circumstances. In our first year we had worked in different teams but were brought together in the same team in the second year. Back then, I was friends with a guy called Valeriy Golovin who was studying in the year above.

All of us were settled in a big gym and the corner designated for girls and cooks (we were five or six people in all) was screened off with a big tarpaulin. In order to prepare breakfast in time, the cooks had to wake up early and also went to bed early. To avoid disturbing them, the rest of the students would disperse in different directions in the evenings. Some played chess or just talked to each other. Through working, relaxing and eating together, we became very close. I don't remember how or who started it, but Kairat and I were nicknamed husband and wife despite the fact that I already had a fiancé of sorts named Valeriy, and he and I would jokingly address each other: "Hey, husband" or "Hey, wife".

We returned to Almaty on the first of September but found that our classes had been postponed due to the absence of the combine operators. Some students went home but I decided to stay because my journey took such a long time. I remember one day when I was just about to go to the reading hall when I saw Kairat coming down the stairs to meet me. He used to be very slim so I was really surprised to see that he had put on weight and asked: " Kairat, what's happened to you?!" It transpired that he had been eating too many of his mother's pies at home!

We enjoyed a jocular friendship but it marked the beginning of a more romantic relationship even though I couldn't take his early courtship seriously. Then the November holidays arrived. Although I was born on November 6th, I celebrated my birthday on the day before, alongside that of another girl. The next day, everyone went home and I was left alone in the room. Kairat was a member of the operational Komsomolsk group that helped the police to maintain order in the students' dormitories during the holidays. He happened to come and see me on my birthday as I was sitting at the long extension table (still unfolded after the party) looking through an album filled with photos of my friends and relatives. I felt very tearful since it was hard being apart from them all on that day.

He positioned himself at one end of the long table and suddenly blurted out: "I don't know how to say this and it's not a joke: I love you". His voice was full of despair but I had finally got the message, loud and clear!

However, prior to this declaration of love, another event had taken place. One of the girls from a higher course and who was also on the construction team, had started to tease Kairat the day before my birthday: "You say that you love Marziya so why are you so hesitant? Why don't you give her a kiss?"

I laughed along with the others but I felt quite worried. Everybody knew that I was engaged to Valeriy Golovin. He had asked me to go with him to Otrar but to be honest, deep down, I didn't take this relationship very seriously. There was no burning passion or a fusion of souls. Although Valeriy was intent on marriage and children, I realized that this would never be more than mere infactuation: a kind of innocent, "puppy", love.

However, at the time when Alma the senior student teased Kairat, I was still very much attached to my boyfriend and had no quarrel with him. That is why when Kairat grabbed me by my arms and kissed me, I felt highly affronted and fighting free of his grasp; slapped his face and ran off in tears.

FEMALE INTUITION

I was irritated when he turned up at my room and hissed: "Go away, Zakiryanov, I don't want you coming here." But one moment later, he declared his love for me and in desperation I decided to take a fresh look at this guy. I had no any special interest in him but I could see that in many ways we were similar and I knew that I could depend on him without fear of being abandoned. I didn't judge him on how he had treated me: it was the beginning of romantic love and a time when any ill- spoken words can hurt a man, ready to fulfil a girl's any wish.

This leads me to a particular story:

After his declaration we often spent time together. One day, when we were having tea in the boys' quarters I, not prone to a sweet tooth, suddenly announced at 11pm "I would love some chocolate!" I didn't notice Kairat leave but shortly afterwards, I heard a knock at my door and there he was, standing with his hand in his pocket and teasing: "Guess what's in my pocket?" He then presented me with giftwrapped *Alenka* chocolate! It turned out that he had taken a taxi to the only grocery store in Stolichniy that was still open so late at night.

My friends often ask me about my secret in being so attractive to men, and my to husband in particular.I think that the most attractive qualities in a woman are sincerity, cheerfulness, femininity and subtle coquetry.

Kairat tends to be emotional and is quick to take offence. During the early years of our courtship, he was very jealous, to the point that I almost broke up with him on several occasions. In some people, jealousy does not diminish their attractiveness but with Kairat, it was awful. If anyone so much as said hello to me, he would grab him by the hand or even worse, his nose, and twist it hard.

These upset me greatly since by nature I am gregarious and enjoy the company of men without there being any alternative agenda. Yes, I like flirting, being playful; it is part of being a woman, but Kairat was forever jumping to conclusions which simply did not exist.

Shortly before we decided to get married, my university friends questioned why I tolerated such extreme jealousy and I myself, began to have serious doubts about our relationship. After one particular scene, I lost patience and declared "Enough is enough! I can't stand any more of this. Let's part as friends before it's too late. Go home and leave me alone!"

He left the Halls, leased to students by the National Economy Institute and located at the junction of Jandosov and Pravda streets, KazSU but by the time he returned two weeks later, we had been relocated to new Halls at 88 Vinogradov Street. Kairat had arrived from Ust Kamenogorsk on the night flight and it took him until six o'clock in the morning to find my new address. In addition to my studies, I was also involved with sport and many social activities and so the minute my head hit the pillow at night, I was sound asleep. That was why my roommates had to answer his knocks rather than me, and they were none too pleased to be woken up so early in the morning.

Opening my door, I greeted him frostily and then fell silent: I was determined to break up with him. He then announced "I'm going to get married." And I replied "Congratulations: Am I invited to your wedding?"

He told me "Of course" and then we both said nothing for a few minutes before he continued "You will be my bride." "What?" I exclaimed "I have no intention of even seeing you anymore".

This was how he proposed marriage and I must admit that it didn't excite me at all. I love Kairat very much but his distrust upset me deeply. Even the day before our wedding with the rings, veil and dress already bought, we had an argument and I was so angry that I threw out this stuff saying: "Take it all away! There'll be no wedding! I don't want to either see you or hear from you ever again!"

We finally found ourselves walking up the stairs of the Almaty Wedding Palace. Khasangaliyev's song "Edem-au" was being played (we have considered it our tune ever since) and we were welcomed by the beaming faces of our friends but I felt my knees tremble and bend. Instead of feeling pleasure and happiness, I was overcome with fear, anxiety and one big question: "What am I doing here?! Perhaps it would be better if I made a run for it: But how? All of our invited guests and my parents are already here."

After I became paralysed, his jealousy abated a little: it was still there but tempered so that there were no longer "scenes" in public.

In the spring 1992 we met a guy, a veteran of the Afghan war, in the residential treatment centre at Saki, Crimea. He also had problems with his legs: one day he was in a wheelchair and the next, on crutches. During treatments, this soldier was often in the same room as me but we never talked. One day as we were exiting the elevator and the Afghan war veteran went off in the opposite direction, I began telling Kairat what I had learned about this guy from the other patients. Before I had finished, Kairat turned and said" He's getting too fond of you!"

Using my woman's intuition, I was aware of the man's interest in me but I was at a loss as to how Kairat had also picked this up!

There was another occasion, at the wedding of the daughter of one of our relatives in Kyrgyzstan, where one of the guests took a shine to me and spent most of the day hanging around me. Noticing early flashes of jealousy emanating from Kairat, I decided to introduce them to each other but I had hardly spoken the words: "Let me introduce my husband…" when this guest immediately interjected: "Who cares who he is!" He then proceeded to compliment me but whatever his intentions, they were quickly squashed by his being persuaded and then forcibly moved to the opposite end of the table!

When a man falls seriously in love with a woman, he tries to win her favour. And it seems to me that if she meets his expectations he will find it very hard to discard his choice, regardless of anything that happens thereafter. Kairat never tires of telling me that when he first saw me serving the table in the student halls, he recognised that I was a woman with good housekeeping skills who would make a good wife. Since childhood I have been very practical, thrifty and keen on cookery but it is never too late for anyone to acquire these skills. However, everything feels pointless if executed with a cold heart.

To be honest, I feel uncomfortable when my husband starts comparing me favourably with movie-star beauties. I fell in love with him simply for who he was. I can't even pinpoint the moment when I realized that this rather unremarkable guy and certainly not the most handsome among my admirers, became my sweetheart.

It had been in love before, but not ardently, and was more interested in focusing on my studies. That is why I felt little remorse about breaking up with Valeriy Golovin, despite his reproaches.

When I returned to Alma-Ata, paralysed, Valeriy was working in KazSU. Someone told him that I had become a wheelchair-bound invalid and although he asked Zina Nazarbekova, one of my classmates, about me he neither phoned nor visited. I found out where he lived but didn't suggest meeting up. What would we have said to each other?

This was during a period of deep despair when I felt especially lonely. How I managed to get out of this situation is a special story.

LONELINESS IS KEENEST
WHEN YOU FEEL ALONE AMONGST MANY PEOPLE

The solution to shifting my deep sense of loneliness appeared in the form of Basya, a Shar-Pei dog which Kairat brought home on New Year's Eve. It took him less than three days to adopt me as his mistress. At first, I was afraid that I might crush him with my wheelchair but we managed fine. After falling asleep on my dressing gown, he woke up and began dragging it towards my bedroom. Halfway there and exhausted, he abandoned it and went off to settle down near my bed. By choosing me above everyone else, this small creature successfully managed to melt the ice in my heart. Ironically, the dog which Kairat found for me had the same proprietous attitude towards me as my husband. As he became older, Baysunkar, or Basya as we called him, demonstrated his devotion towards me by being very protective, especially when anyone approached my wheelchair. On one occasion, he even bit Kairat, leaving a mark in the shape of the letter"Ц". Kairat took it in good humour and jokingly boasted to his friends that this sign from Basya was a prediction that he would become a most noble man.

Sadly my Basya was poisoned when we moved into the first of two houses which I built. Prior to that, he had been stolen. It was a real tragedy! When he went missing, both the children and Kairat, on his return from work, repeatedly combed the holiday village where we were staying. I was so distraught that I was on the point of bursting into tears. It was late October and time for us to return to our town house. All of our stuff was packed and it was already ten o'clock at night. We felt that we were marking time waiting for Basya to come back; it would have been terrible if he appeared and found nobody at home. Suddenly, as Baurzhan was drawing the blinds, he turned to me and exclaimed: "Mum, I think Basya is back!" We listened carefully but everything was quiet until we heard a faint scratching noise at the door. Basya had indeed returned but he was now carrying a huge chain around his neck and had been so badly beaten up that he was too exhausted to even bark.

This spring, Basya will have been dead for six years. He had a very loud and penetrating bark and we suspect that this might have led our neighbours to poison him. However, it would be wrong to blame anyone in particular since we don't know exactly what happened. One day Basya simply couldn't get up. Kairat and I took him to the animal clinic where he was diagnosed as having been poisoned. It happened in the morning and in the afternoon I visited a friend, having agreed with the vet that we would return that night.

But at six o'clock in the evening I felt worried and decided to call Kairat. As a rule he didn't finish work until seven or eight but that night he managed to wind things up early and we rushed over to the clinic. Basya was on a drip and as we approached, calling "Basya! Basya!" he raised his head a little and collapsed. He had been waiting until we came: my Basya died in front of my very eyes.

We buried him in the neighbourhood of Talgara, close to where I was building the sports stadium and Kaymar was finishing building the new hotel for the Academy of Sports and Tourism. As we laid him to rest, the rain poured down as though nature was mourning Basya with me.

Since then, I have developed a great empathy with dog owners who become so completely devoted to their pets that they consider them part of the family. After my Basya died and despite encouragement from my husband, I decided that I would never keep another dog. Any dog after Basya, would have felt too much like a stranger.

I KNEW I HAD FOUND MY SOULMATE
AS SOON AS I SAW HER

Kairat Zakiryanov

I am self-made man. However they say that behind every successful man is a successful woman and this is certainly true in my case.

I can't pretend that Marziya and I dated in our first year at University: I admired her from a distance but was too shy to approach her.

After school I applied to study at the Novosibirsk state university but I missed out by a half a point. Exams in the top institutes of higher education in the Soviet Union were sat a month earlier than elsewhere and this arrangement guaranteed outstanding students their first choice of University places.

So I came to Almaty and applied to the Faculty of Mechanics and Mathematics of KazSU. My second cousin Khazif Khisamiev being very practical said: "Stay at my place but apply for a room in the student halls. Otherwise they may say that since you weren't living here when you enrolled, you won't be eligible for student accommodation."

I got authorization and the supervisor showed me where I would be living. I made my bed, said goodbye to the guys and then walking along the corridor, I suddenly recognised my soulmate. She was talking to somebody, with lively gesticulations. During the run up to the exams I went to her Halls several times hoping to see her but I wasn't lucky.

We got to know each other better when we became students even though she had enrolled in another faculty. Marziya was practical in all respects (she expertly repairs plugs and irons in our house); she chose computing mathematics whilst I in my turn, opted for algebra and number theory.

Whilst studying, I only once got a "C"; a low grade presented for theoretical mechanics by Maruan Nadirkhanovich Sagitov, Faculty Dean, due to the fact that when we started seeing each other, I could barely be apart from Marziya for even one minute.

This was in the third year, at the beginning of our love affair. We had changed our halls and moved to 57, Zhandosov. We had previously lived on different floors and had different friends but by then, we were sharing the same floor and had mutual friends from our involvement in the construction team. This brought us even closer together and the "C" grade was a mark of our love in full swing!

We met after classes but even during the most important lectures, I engineered ways of communicating with her, by passing notes or whispering. She didn't mind but the Dean was always keeping a watch over his students and would frequently be impelled to shout out: "Zakiryanov, get up", « Zakiryanov, stop talking", "Zakiryanov, get out." I now understand why he reacted like this: I have been giving lectures for seven years and when any of my students don't pay attention, it feels like a slap in the face.

Nowadays, it is hard to find a couple who haven't had intimate relations prior to their wedding but although we had been together for two years, we were not united in the conjugal sense until our marriage had been registered. I was not opposed to this but Marziya had inherited strong moral principles from her family.

I am sorry to admit that I am a man affected by pathological jealousy. I understand why Marziya was even on the point of divorcing me. If someone greeted her or complimented her, I immediately made a scene. Perhaps it's a sign of my lack of confidence...

I AM SORRY THAT I WAS NOT A DAUGHTER
TO MY MOTHER-IN-LAW

I have enjoyed a happy marriage but the feeling of bitterness which stems from my husband's parents' negligence of our marriage has remained with me throughout. My father died in May 1980, and I, his beloved daughter, got married five years earlier. And during these years he never once visited my husband's native land , as father of their daughter-in-law. My parents never blamed me or Kairat for this.

Both my father-in-law and my mother-in-law were good people. If they hadn't been so, my husband would never have inherited all of his fine qualities: everyone who met him remarked upon his sincerity. But many years on, I am still left wondering what made them spurn centuries'old traditions. As far as I was aware, they bore no ill feelings towards either me or their son and he had behaved in a way that would have pleased any parent, by choosing a bride from a respectable Kazakh family. They didn't come to my parents to ask them for my hand in marriage and nor did they even write or call them. Allegedly, circumstances had prevented them from doing any of this and they suggested that they could wait until the wedding to get to know my parents. My family comes from a region in Kazakhstan where customs are highly respected and it is normal for an entire neighborhood to be made aware of an impending marriage by watching the bride's family preparing thier house for a visit from their future son-in-law's parents. With apologises for speaking ill of my late mother-in-law, I asked her: "Mum, why are you upsetting us? It is not a good thing to follow some of the old traditions and celebrate a wedding in the simplest way, if this makes the couple happy?"

In our community, even the smallest actions are important when honouring tradition and our elders. This is why, when my father-in-law and then my mother-in-law fell ill, I unquestioningly fulfilled my duty as a daughter-in-law to go and look after them.

Ironically, all of Kairat's brothers married to Russian girls. However, when it came to the marriages of her daughters, my mother-in-law's attitude was far from indifferent: "We are shala-Kazakh from East Kazakhstan and it is important that these ceremonies are organised properly: After all, the manner in which a bride enters her husband's home has an impact upon her status in her new family. And she added with meaning: a girl treads a narrow path." Kairat's mother had heard a lot about situations where a bride's parents, having attended a wedding arranged by the groom's relatives, returned home feeling insulted by the manner in which Shala-Kazakh had received them. It is a pity that my mother-in-law only reflected on such things shortly before she died: had she considered her treatment of me earlier, she would probably have gained another daughter.

I hope that people don't misunderstand me. I certainly don't support the notion that in order to observe wedding customs, parents take out huge loans which then take them five or six years to repay pay off : Debts can lead to conflict and even divorce. I stand for the preservation of customs that are inherent to Kazakhs and for which we are respected all over the world: consideration of family values, compassion for our elders and children, and tolerance and respect towards foreigners. I have little to do with politics but I like to think that these values distinguish Kazakhstan from other countries in Central Asia, with the result that our country is often claimed to be the bridge between the East and the West.

MY WIFE WAS BORN TO SUFFER

Kairat Zakiryanov

It is possible that if the accident of 1991 hadn't happened, we would have split up. I was annoyed, even angry about her youth Maximalism. I was also unhappy with her criticism of my family: surely she could just have ignored her grievances concerning her perception of their flaws, rather than aggravating the situation by focusing her attention on them. This led to more and more arguments until I was on the point of divorcing her.

Fate brought us back together and it felt as though our misfortune forced us to overcome severe trials and hold our family together. It was effective but at the sacrifice of Marziya's health.

When she fell seriously ill in autumn 2012, I visited a well-known healer. It was difficult to get an appointment but I hoped that she would be able to help Marziya. According to the healer, my wife had been brought into this world with a special mission to suffer for her relatives.

What am I talking about? I will try to explain the reason behind the sublime relationship I had with Marziya. That romantic love which sprung forth when I was seventeen years old developed over our many years together, into something more spiritual and I never tire of repeating that it is hard to find anyone else like Marziya on our earth. When she became unable to walk, I wasn't overly discomforted. There was no question of us hiring someone to prepare meals or do the laundry. It was simply not part of the agenda. My wife refused to be assisted. She declared that she could manage everything by herself and despite being confined to a wheelchair; she learned how to wash, iron, and cook, in addition to bringing up the children, entertaining guests and immersing herself in my affairs.

But at what cost and what was her ultimate goal?

My colleagues understood my situation and made few demands, especially during the first few months following the accident when I was unable to work full time. But after a while, I was able to spend even more time at work than them because Marziya not only just empathized with my work but was also so bound up in it.

Here is a simple example. Both of us are mathematicians. When we moved to Ust Kamenogorsk, I earned 125 roubles but she earned more than double, plus bonuses. All our professors took on additional work at the nearby institute of higher education in order to supplement their low incomes but because of Marizya, I had no need to do likewise and was therefore free to concentrate on my academic career and ambition to become a head of department.

We always had lunch and dinner together and guests were always warmly welcomed by my wife. I could focus on my work that I loved so much. In my search for rare books I would do the rounds of second-hand bookshops and then work on my thesis till three or four in the morning.

Ours names are as inseparable from each other as the physicists Pierre Curie and Maria Sklodovskaya. Both of them were devoted to science and have gone down in history as a couple of two outstanding, talented people who granted mankind remarkable scientific discoveries. There are numerous other examples of famous couples who shared a special, spiritual and unifying force: Leo Tolstoy and his selfless wife Sofya Andreevna, Majit Begalin and Olesya Ivanova, Mikhail Romm and Elena Kuzmina....

Marziya was also able to offer practical help in the making of my professional career. When I was a post -graduate student at the Institute of Mathematics of the Siberian branch of the Academy of Sciences of the USSR, I struggled with one very interesting problem. In order to obtain the theorem of full value, I lacked one contrary instance. I needed to set up a matrix to support all my hypotheses. I went through hundreds and thousands of options but I was unable to find the necessary parameter. One day Marziya remarked: "You are spending far too much time on writing and calculating: perhaps it would be better to create a computer programme to process this data?" Unconvinced, I asked her to give it a try and then left for Novosibirsk. I called at the Halls where I usually stayed and the warden passed me a note. It transpired that Marziya had already succeeded in writing a computer programme which had found a matrix to support my theory.

I was honoured to have the completed theorem published in one of Moscow's most serious journals "Mathematical Notes": something which my colleagues could only dream about!

In contrast to me, Marziya is very faithful to her religion. What is the difference between us and the Muslim Brotherhood – Arabs? They don't respect aruakhs and we believe firmly that the souls of our ancestors can support us in moments of crises.

She is also very devoted to her ancestors. Even if she's on a short visit to her home town in Temir , she will always make a point of going to the cemetery where she will call out in a loud voice: "Mum, Dad, Grandma, Grandpa, Aunt, I've come to see you. Can you hear me?"

Whenever I set out to solve large problems or to defend myself from any attacks on my character, she always repeated: "You neither stole anything nor killed anyone. The Aruakhs know this and they will support you. But you must believe in them!"

And I began to think that she could be right! Of course I had the support of friends as well as Marziya but each time information was presented to suggest that I had been involved in criminal activity and I had to face my investigators, all of them, for some reason, turned from being my opponents to my defenders.

I recall one incident that illustrates clearly her honesty and moral purity. While living in Ust Kamenogorsk and working in Vostokkazgeologiya, she earned a much higher salary than me but it was not easy money. Her day began at six in the morning and juggling work with the care of two small children, she was so exhausted by ten at night that she fell asleep the minute her head hit the pillow.

So when I was elected as pro-rector, I decided to make things easier for her by asking the pro-rector of the construction and road institute to offer her a less taxing job. My colleague then asked Mukhtar Kitapbayev, Head of Higher Mathematics to process this request and Marziya was told that the job would be hers as soon as a vacancy became available. Her friend Zinat (Zinka) who was employed as a part-time lecturer dreamed of attaining a full-time post but now all of a sudden, Marziya Nurtazovna Zakiryanova had been offered the job instead.

When Kitapbayev called Marziya to ask her to fill in an application, my wife felt so bad about jumping the queue as a result of my connections and effectively usurping her friend, that she made the condition that she would only accept a position if any became available after Zinat had been offered the first job that came up.

And that is typical of Marziya: consistently loyal to her friends and principles.

EVERYTHING IS WITHIN YOUR POWER

If true love exists between spouses, it can't be forsaken. My love for my husband is the same as that which I feel for my children and I want to forever cherish him.

There was a time when Kairat was so absorbed by his work that I began to feel that he had drifted apart from not only me but also, from the family. My solution was to drag him out for long walks and use this time to sort out our relationship. Neither he nor I can tolerate insincerity and any arguments were so emotionally fired that you would think

92

that we were Italian! But as we grew older, we became calmer, perhaps because we had accepted at last that we could trust each other and more importantly, realised just how much we meant to each other. By then, we could anticipate each other's every movement and expression.

We could also not afford to spend time arguing when so many other matters demanded our attention, especially our work and children.

It was in February 1992 when my seemingly infinite operations (four in all) came to an end. I was still young and of course I tormented myself with all sorts of notions whenever Kairat worked late into the night at his office, despite the fact that I had always known this to be a compulsory part of his job. At that time the East Kazakhstan University was visited by many dignitaries from Almaty, and as senior pro-rector, Kairat was responsible for both work-related meetings and afterwards, their entertainment. It was a common practice in any provincial town.

Before my accident I worked as the lecturer and I was well aware that in such environments, there were many women and girls who were both beautiful and single. Late at night when I heard the front door open I tried not to show my husband that I was upset by smiling and adopting a cheerful tone of voice. I repeatedly tried to find comfort by telling myself:"Marziya, remember that even able- bodied women are not immune to their husbands' infidelity but you have no concrete reason to think that your husband is being unfaithful."

I had a lot of friends in both of the universities of Ust Kamenogorsk but nobody ever mentioned anything about Kairat having another woman on the side. One close friend who worked alongside Kairat always kept me up to date with the all University events and although I never showed any interest in gossip, I was so worried, that I began to look for clues about things which I really wished to avoid.

I tried to calm myself: "Don't sulk, don't complain, and don't go overboard: trust in the grace of God and let everything be as it should be." During the long evenings I prayed in the kitchen: "God the Almighty, give me strength. I commit myself to your care. I have no any desire to force anybody to stay with me."

Having reached this point, I felt calmer but still felt that I had to express my feelings to Kairat and so, on one of our Sunday walks, told him: "It's not our fault that any of this has happened to us. You are still young but even though I am disabled I couldn't bear to see you with another woman as long as we're living together."

He didn't allow me to finish and retorted: "What on earth are you talking about?!"

I didn't want to turn this conversation into the argument, but I was obsessed with re-opening the discussion and a few months later when we were again on a walk, brought up the matter again. On that ocassion, my husband listened to me without interrupting.

By then, autumn 1992, we had received a full diagnosis which made it clear that I would never recover the use of my legs

"If you have any flings rather than serious love affairs I would like to be the first to know. I feel that I could overcome a split in our relationships but treachery would kill me. I will let you go, and ask only that you support your children. If you are concerned about rumours that you abandoned your disabled wife, I will do everything in my power to ensure that no-one dares to lay the blame at your door. If none of this happens, then I will work on convincing people that everything is fine and as it should be."

And he replied: "Your wheelchair is of no consequence to me: you are the same person as you were before. I have never met anyone who is as dear to me as you are. I don't want anyone else. Please, stop torturing yourself and me with such thoughts".

For the second time that day, I prayed: "God the Almighty, I commit myself to your care".

And now, that I have been given a diagnosis which I cannot survive, I address a third message to God: "God, I will try anything to survive this hell but I commit myself to your care as usual. Please help me"...

SHE WAS CAST FROM THE SAME MOULD AS YOU!

At the risk of tempting fate, I must admit that we are a very happy family. There are never any disagreements even on trivial matters concerning matchmaking, children or our grandsons.

But building good relationships within the family requires a great deal of patience, especially when the children are ready to leave home.

Happily I was smart and strong enough to appreciate the importance of maintaining a calm atmosphere. The only time that voices were raised or became over- excited was when my husband and I were addressing each other and this was mainly unavoidable, given our personalities.

Over twenty years ago, just like Baron Munchausen, I dragged myself out of a very stressful situation, thanks largely to the stimulation of my children Baurzhan and Aselya. Now my children have their own families. Both our daughter-in-law and our son-in-law have proved to be open-hearted people.

When Baurzhan first told us that he had fallen in love with a Russian girl named Sveta, I tried to convince him that cultural differences would make it hard for her to become accustomed to our Kazakh traditions. And what was my son's reply? "Oh, there's no need to worry about that, Mum: she was made from the same mould as you!" Because of his girlfriend, he didn't want to leave Ust Kamenogorsk when we moved to Almaty in 1997 but how I could leave him behind? I explained to him that I needed his help; Kairat spent all day at work and although I had learned to do many things by myself, I didn't feel totally confident and I still required assistance, for example, to get to the bathroom. But to be honest, the real reason that I wanted my son to stay with me was for my own peace of mind. I was worried that left alone, he would be susceptible to the alcohol and drug abuse which had rapidly spread amongst our country's youth after the fall of the "Iron Curtain." I did however, promise that he could visit his girlfriend and that she could come and stay with us and enjoy sightseeing in Almaty.

It was the right decision: They didn't stop being friends and their teenage romance led to marriage. When Baurzhan decided to marry Sveta, my friends appealed to me: « Marziya, you shouldn't allow this". But I decided that if my son believed that this was the best girl that he had ever met, then so be it.

Sveta, the mother of our grandsons, has proved herself a fine person and my Russian daughter-in-law has no problem in observing Kazakh traditions, including the preparation of meat Kazakh - style and cooking sheep's heads for guests of honour.

Tamerlan, my eldest grandson, aspires to gain a perfect knowledge of the language of his people. Nowadays this is quite easy because he can speak to boys of his age who know Kazakh. As he was growing up, I used to tell him: "Tamosya, don't worry if you don't speak it perfectly, we can correct you, but if you're too timid to practice your native language, you'll never be any good at it."

Given his strong interest in our country, his response to the naming of his brother came as no surprise. When Baurzhan's youngest boy was born at the end of October 2012, my son decided that he and his wife would name him themselves. Tamerlan and my granddaughter Tomiris had both been named by us and even this time, Kairat was determined to have it his own way, proposing that the child be named Tanar, after the Turkic God Tengri. I told him not to meddle, asking him: "How many children are they expected to have before they're free to choose their own name?!" When Tamoska came round to our house, we asked him what his parents had decided to call his brother and he replied: "Oh, grandma, they went through a whole list of stupid names, such as Artur and Rolan

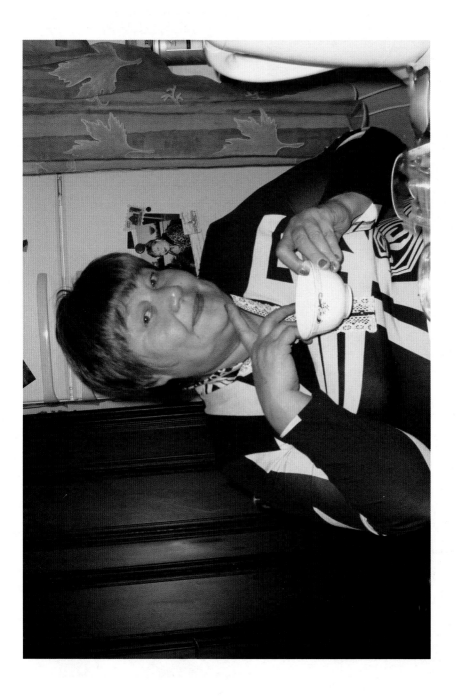

Almaty, Bauma groove, M.Sagitov Dean of MechMat fac. at KAZGU, congratulates me with 1st place on traditional race

Our Wedding, 30th of October, 1975

In building troop, Tulgay region, 1979

With my classmates, Temir town

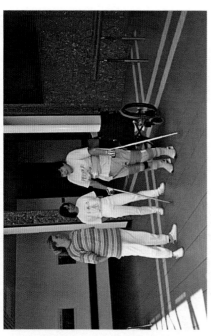

Kairat and his parents

In hospital Bayreuth , Germany 1995

Having fun with my friends

Kairat presents a new Sports Museum,
to our President in Almaty. 2000

The President of Kazakhstan and my husband presentation
of Kazakh-American Free University (Ust-Kamenogorsk, 1995)

Meeting the President N.Nazarbayev in VKGU
Ust-Kamenogorsk, 1995)

Cheers with our first Lady of Kazakhstan S.Nazarbayeva
and Minister of Education K.Kusherbayev (December, 1998)

Kairat with his brothers in Karatkul

Kairat with Ministries of Education of USSR and Kazakhstan with Governor of East Kazakhstan province

Kairat presents his book at the Royal Geographic Society (London, 2012)

Kairst's friend Bagdat Shayakhmetov celebration 55th Birthday

Four generation from "sheshe" to grandson

I am a gourmet

My Birthday

Karlovy Vary, with the brave soldier "Shweik"

My son Baurzhan and Swetlana Wedding (Almaty, 1997)

My daughter Asel and Mars Wedding (Bishkek, 2001)

In Actobe with my mother And relatives

Our home garden

With my daughter Asel

With my son Baurzhan

With Arslan

With Danat

With Tamerlan

With Ruslan

With Tomiris

Farida's summer house – "dacha", 2013

My helpers: Abay, Nurkanat, Ilzira, Lera and Talgat

I like my weelchair

With my dog "Bas'ka – Baisunkar"

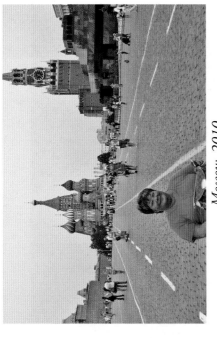

Moscow, 2010

In front of Roman Colosseum, 2010

Hong-Kong, 2009

Venice, 2010

In Egypt. Relaxing and fishing in Red sea, enjoying ageless Pyramids

In Arab Emirates, Persian Gulf

Kairat always carries me in his arms

This how I dive into the pool

Indian ocean

I like water-based recreation

Paris, Louver, 2010

August 2013. With Children Asel and Baurzhan

Visiting Siberian lakes

In Capitoline Museum in Rome. Italy, 2010

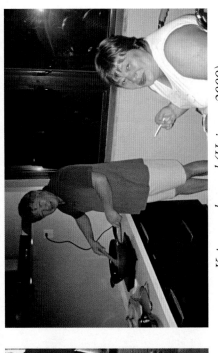

Hainan, 2009

Kairat cooks meal (Hainan, 2009)

My Birthday in Paris

My Family

instead of just going for a normal Kazakh name but you'll be pleased to hear that they eventually decided upon Danat."

My daughter-in-law hasn't accepted our religion but when something goes wrong Sveta, hesitant about going alone, will usually come to me with the suggestion: "Mum, don't you think it would be a good idea if we were to visit to mosque?" And one day, when I was approaching the house which we shared, I heard her reading aloud the Sura from the Koran. I had advised her if you have a heavy heart, turn to the Koran and you will be able to cleanse your aura.

...When a girl becomes the wife of her son, many a mother-in-law is prone to demand too much of her: expecting her to be smarter, more dexterous and nimble, without stopping to consider the fact that she is as young and inexperienced as the son and is either able to do something, or not. If you consent to your son's marriage, you should accept the daughter-in-law as she is and then gently try to re-educate her in the ways of your household. This should be a gradual process which nurtures mutual understanding, rather than a regime in which orders are issued. Otherwise, the mother-in-law is likely to alienate her daughter-in-law and achieve nothing.

In order to help my children establish their own relationship, independent of us, I built another house for Kairat and me. When we moved out, my grandchildren were distraught and my young granddaughter Tomirisk beseeched me: "Grandma, grandma, why are you moving into this other house? I want us to carry on living together!" As a rule, it's usually the daughter-in-law who doesn't want to live with her husband's parents but in our case, it was Baurzhan, rather than Sveta, who found it harder to live with us. I understood completely, his reasons for wanting his freedom: he was very independent and wilful and was unable to really feel like the head of his own household until he had a place of his own.

They set about organising the rooms in their house in accordance to their own plans and tried to establish their own domestic arrangements. With all good intentions, I was determined not to interfere and told them: "Only God knows, but you may be burdened with me in old age so in the meantime, I want you to enjoy your own lives without having to care for us." However, like it or not, the fact remains that parents will always be aware of when troubles arise in their children's lives! We have now been living in separate houses for six years and though I try not to impose upon them, if I ever need help, Sveta will respond immediately.

Baurzhan, being male, needs a few reminders!

My Asel's family is another source of joy for me. She met Mars in Issyk Kul during a family holiday but two years later, we decided to send her abroad to study. Hearing this, Mars declared that if she went, he would consider it the end of their relationship. Tears and assurances from Asel that the distance wouldn't affect their feelings had no effect and so my daughter decided to listen to her heart and stayed with Mars. As far as I know, she has never regretted it. Both Kairat and I love our son-in-law. Mars is very responsible, independent and mature beyond his years, probably because he lost his father at a young age and had to take on the role of head of his family. Being someone who loves talking, I learned how to speak his language and greatly enjoy discussing many subjects with him including politics, psychology and children.

My daughter's family has recently moved to Bishkek but Asel and our two grandsons often visit us. Mars fully understands and supports these visits since he knows how important they are for us. As soon as they come in the door, Baurzhan's children rush over to our place and our lives are immediately filled with joyful disorder.

… My own father was at the Front when he fell in love with a Russian girl who was working as a nurse. After the war he asked for his parents' consent to bring her home but they refused. My father was deeply upset and downed a few drinks, blaming them for ruining his happiness but he had no option but to accept their decision. I can imagine that when she learned about this, my mother wasn't too happy but being woman of Eastern culture she didn't show her disapproval.

When my children chose spouses of different ethnic origins I remembered my father. Out of respect for his parents he turned away from his first love. However, when he fell in love with a woman of another ethnic origin for a second time, my strict grandparents, fearing that their unacceptance of this union would destroy his life, gave their consent. With reference to such history, how could I ever have prevented either of my children from marrying whoever they chose?

MY SON SPEAKS OF MY AMAZING CHARIZMA

Kairat Zakiryanov

My son has been married for sixteen years. At their wedding anniversary Marziya thanked our daughter-in-law, who she thought of as her own daughter, for giving all of the children Kazakh names: Tamerlan, Tomiris, and Danat. While Baurzhan spent have seven years studying in Europe, Sveta lived with us and never once asked to go to a party or stay over at a friend's place. Thanks to Sveta, we maintained a special, close bond with our son's family despite his absence.

When Marziya broke her leg in the summer 2011, I was afraid that she wouldn't live to see the spring and organized the shooting of a documentary film about our family. There is a section in which my son speaks about me and I was surprised to hear that he credits me with having such amazing charisma that I can turn enemies into friends!

I was not a perfect father and was often quick to use punches in response to my son's problems with schoolwork. One day, when Baurzhan was a child, he brought home a pile of stuff which he had taken from a shop. When he admitted what he had done, I slapped his face and dragging him by the hand back to the shop, made him apologize to the shopkeeper. I must confess that any of my children's or grandchildren's bad qualities are inherited from me: like it or not, children and grandchildren will naturally imitate their father.

I remember one incident from my childhood. My neighbour Shurka Skorojenin, who was three years older than me, had come along to one of the dances at the Technical School. Bored, he was ready to leave and looking over at the group of younger boys, he invited me to accompany him. I was proud to have been picked out and gladly went with him. However, when we arrived at his place, Shurka plunged his hand into the water barrel and brought out a half-litre bottle of vodka! He splashed some vodka into a facetted glass and told me to drink.

My parents had instructed me never to drink alcohol. Regardless of my feelings of trepidation and the other boy's perceived hold over me, I would have flatly refused the vodka if I hadn't reminded myself that often adults don't always practice what they preach. In this instance, I happened to remember my father returning from a distant pasture so inebriated that he could barely ride his horse. And so, following the rule that we mimic our parents' behaviour, both good and bad, I drank up and my first acquaintance with alcohol ended with me hanging around the streets until 4am and throwing up on every corner.

But returning to our children: When Asel told us that she was going to marry Mars, a man from a different ethnic background, I tried to reason with her: "You should continue with your studies. Arrangements have already been made for you to do your Masters in London and I'm sure that this period apart will only prove your feelings for each other." However our daughter had already made up her mind. On many occasions, returning home from visiting our grandchildren in Bishkek, I admit that I've teased my wife by saying: "Just think; if our daughter had listened to me and then married instead, a Kazakh from Atirau, you would be able to jump in the car and be with them in three hours, hugging your grandchildren!"

When we learned about Marziya's recent diagnosis, she immediately appealed to God: "What have I done wrong?! Why I have I had to endure such misfortune?"

I then tried to comfort her by saying: " You should thank God that after the accident you were given the chance to enjoy to life to the full for twenty one years, allowing you to rear and educate two beautiful and remarkable children."

These were particularly poignant words since my son had revealed to me that without the support of his mother, he could easily have become addicted to drugs and as a consequence, turned to crime. I was more than aware that without Marziya, things could have turned out very differently especially since during his adolescence, the long hours which I was required to work as Vice Rector of the East Kazakhstan State University meant that I was rarely at home.

GRANDMA CAN PULL OUT PHOTOGRAPHS OF HER GRANDCHILDREN FASTER THAN A COWBOY CAN DRAW HIS PISTOL!

Our grandchildren express their feelings for us in the form of poems, timed to mark different events.

In 2008 when Kairat received the unexpected news that he had been elected a full member of the prestigious Petrovsky Academy of Sciences and Arts, established in the 18th century by Peter the First, our eldest grandson Tamerlan-Tamosya proudly wrote him a poem that included the following lines:

My grandpa is the brightest person.
He proved Genghis Khan to be an indigenous Kazakh.

In addition he is the king of mathematics
And has now become a full member of the Petrovsky Academy.
It was not easy to be selected as a member, even by well-known academics from Moscow.

Tamerlan was very proud of his grandfather's successes and attached great importance to the fact that his grandfather, following the launch of his book "Under the Wolf's Nest: A Turkic Rhapsody" was invited to present a lecture at Cambridge University.

Here is one of the poems written by Tamerlan for my birthday:
My beloved grandma, happy birthday!
You are 55 years old!
Each day of your life is full of joyful emotion,
Nobody is bored with you.
We love you so much.

The following year he penned me another message:
There is one person,
She is so different.
She taught me to be fair
And to avoid doing bad things.
And now she is only 56 years old.
She could climb a mountain.

By that time I had finished building houses, it was my intention to get involved in any business which would earn me a million. And I could have done it had I not fallen ill. When Tamerlan wrote that "she could climb a mountain" he meant that I would be able to get back on my feet.

I am always very surprised to see a child express so clearly, thoughts and conclusions which some adults struggle to process. But the most important, simple word which he includes in each of his poems is "love".

My grandma, happy birthday!
I wish you happiness, joy and fun,
Let your friends who love you so much
Invite you to take a cup of tea with them.
You'll get enviable health,

This year was rather hard for you.
Clenching your teeth you felt you could overcome everything -
Pain and misfortune.
Now it's completely disappeared, like a nightmare,
Which never returns.
Today you're so beautiful.
You're a wonderful person,
You're supportive and understanding.
And if anything needs to be cooked
You're the master chef.
If you really needed to, you might catch a wild boar.
Your soul is spring's abode.
In this world you are like guardian angel.
Following your advice,
Any person will be dear.
There are not enough stars in the sky to describe
How big my love is.
And just summing up I will repeat again
Happy Birthday to You!

He inherited his poetic soul from his grandfather. Kairat used to sing his favourite songs whenever he wanted to convey his feelings for me and it was partly because of this that I fell in love with him. He regularly visited the fifth year students with whom I kept company and on one occasion sat down beside my bed and picking up his guitar sang:

Pearls in your hair,
Emeralds in your eyes,
Everything reminds me of a fairy-tale,
In the light in your eyes.

Thus, he ensured that he captured my attention: none of my other admirers were as sincere and nor could any of them sing! I myself can't sing and so Kairat's performance in the front of everybody impressed me all the more.

Our older grandson knowing that, decided to devote poem on the subject to Kairat:

He is proud to be a part of his clan.
And who would have thought he could also sing.
Whatever goal he had in mind, he achieved it.
Today he is happy and loved.
He became a mathematician and wrote books.
And he gave much to his children,
They are charmed with his nobility.
He is held in high esteem but is a hero
In the eyes of his family.
I cannot describe
How great is my love
But words are nothing since
Love is best conveyed through deeds.

I have a natural affinity with Arslan, Asel's older son and this sometimes bothers my daughter who feels that I sometimes neglect Rusya a little. To this I reply that all of grandchildren are loved equally and if any of them appear to be favoured, it is probably Rusya and Tomiris since it is not unusual for adults to pamper the youngest!

Below is the poem written by Tamerlan and Arslan for our thirty fifth wedding anniversary:

Grandma and grandpa: Congratulations to you.
We hope life brings you joy, fun and love.
You've been together for 35 years.
And we hope that it's not the half of it
You will stay together, in love with each other.
You're loved from above
As the best family.
You always help and remember your relatives.
Your acts are selfless and the love between you is pure.
Loving each other,
You have recurring and passionate discussions
Dears, thank you for our families.
This poem is devoted to you in all sincerity.
We wish you a long and happy life.

These words were addressed personally from Arslan:
Your wedding anniversary
It's always fun for your grandchildren.
Congratulations to you, grandma and grandpa,
We wish you long and happy life.
We give you our hugs.
We treat you as our friends,
We love coming to visit you at your place.
Playing different games
And being filled with grandma's pies
Each child can't ask for anything more.
We love you so much,
We can never hurt you.
Let your life be long
And full with happy days forever.

This is one of their poems for my birthday:

Congratulations from your beloved grandson:
My grandma: happy birthday.
Let your life be long
So that you can always watch over me.
Today I would like to say,
That you're the best of the best.
You're wonderful
May you live to be three hundred years old.

All of these words made my endurance of even the most difficult situations worthwhile. Here is one poem by my granddaughter Tomiris:

I love you, grandma.
I would like to be with you always
Morning, noon and night
Nothing could ever prevent me from seeing you
I will love you no matter what the season
Winter, spring, fall…
If anyone asks: who is the most beautiful?
The answer is simple:
My grandma; my only grandma.
I am your princess and you are my queen.
Is there anybody as beautiful as you are?
Of course: no- one.
My grandma!
I love you so much.

Tamerlan-Tamosy wants me to celebrate my next birthday with him:

Happiness can't be without tears.
But overcoming this pain,
You endure it without giving any sign.
Who knows what would have happened
If our grandma hadn't been with us.
What would we do?
Me, Asel, grandpa?
You have devoted your life to us all.
Perhaps that's not all,
Maybe you have given us more than your life.
Without you I wouldn't be here,
And instead, would be milking goats somewhere in Poland.
Not very often
But when I am praying, I'm asking God:
"Give her strength,
And let her hear me say, in another year
My beloved grandma: happy birthday."

"Milking goats somewhere in Poland"? My grandson has a good sense of humour! Baurzhan studied in the Czech Republic. We thought that he might stay there.

Arslan, Aselya's son, is keen on football, as well as writing poetry. In order to train he has to get up very early but he never needs to be woken up and gets very upset if for any reason, he misses it. He is such a big fan of this sport that even his younger brother Ruslan has started taking a great interest in it.

Our Aselya's eldest son is distinguished by his tactfulness or as Kairat puts it, his political correctness: he is able to size up a situation very quickly and then respond accordingly. Each of my grandchildren is unique and they are the best anesthetic I could ever wish for. When I'm with them or even just looking at them, I feel my soul blossom. This is what keeps me going!

I'll try my best to stay with them and I need to bring up Danat, my youngest grandchild. My four grandchildren have received my lessons for life but I still have so many more things to share with them.

ONE OF LIFE'S GREAT MISSIONS: INSTILING MORALITY IN OUR DESCENDANTS

When Asel comes to Almaty with her children, we immediately take on board all that they are. Generally speaking, they are allowed to do whatever they want and we enjoy watching them jumping, hopping, shouting and playing war with *atashka* (grandfather). I just ask them not to break anything! Then the toys are put away and I their *apashka* will set the table with numerous tasty dishes

The grandchildren know that I will not ask them to do anything without a reason and from early on, I have illustrated why anything is prohibited by example. Thus, in order to explain why they shouldn't go near the fire or cooker etc., I explained to them that they could get burned and then, for a fraction of a second, made them touch the hot surface with their finger.

Similarly, they were told to be careful not to break dishes since they would either cut themselves or their dear apashka would fall and break apart like a fragile vase when gathering up the shards.

Their confidence in me owes much to the esteem in which I am held by other adults: relatives, friends and of course, the anxious love expressed by their grandfather. They realize that no one earns or deserves such love and respect without good reason.

You may ask how I gained such an understanding of the relationships between parents, children and grandparents. As grandparents, we are invested with a great responsibility when a young couple starts a family. As new graduates still inexperienced in their fields, they have to prove themselves at work and make their names in society, concurrent with running a home and undertaking domestic duties such as preparing meals, buying clothes, taking the children to kindergarten or school and assisting them with their homework. It is not surprising that they have no energy and time for conversation. Much of the children's upbringing is undertaken by kindergarten nursery nurses and schoolteachers or in the worst case scenario, by company they meet on the streets.

However, amidst of all this, it is important that children feel valued by their parents. When my children were born, their grandparents lived far away so it was up to me to make time to speak to them and to make them feel important members of the family. I therefore made sure that I conversed with them on a regular basis; asking them about kindergarten or school, their friends and romantic feelings. Intimate bonds between parents and their children are particularly close in the early years when children are happy to talk about anything but with adolescence, they become more hesitant about answering questions and tend to bury their feelings, and this is the period when special effort is required to keep channels of communication open. Naturally, I try not to fuss over my children or treat them like babies but I still continue to educate them by means of conversation. They have always had a maturity which has enabled them to vociferously articulate their problems to me and this is a reason why they are so saddened by my terrible diagnosis.

The eldest grandchild Tamerlan once remarked: "Apashka it's so obvious to everyone how much you and atashka love each other!"

This made me very happy since it made me realize how important it is for my grandchildren to acknowledge the love which exists between their grandparents despite the fact that they argue from time to time. And love isn't recognized though words alone.

... In the future, they will build their own families based on our pattern and a canon of their own family life will again be the need for open communication and intimate conversation so that the young can learn about the positive and the negative sides of life, base and noble actions, and good and bad courses of action.

GRANDFATHER'S "DAUGHTER"

It's more than twenty years since I changed from a vivacious young woman who liked bright dresses and high heeled shoes into a disabled invalid and I often try to analyze what equipped me to manage the physical and psychological pain. I have finally come to the conclusion that the foundations of my childhood played a large part.

Even though I was born into an ordinary family (my mother dealt with trade and my father worked in the militia and later the Road department), we had a lot of books at home.

My illiterate *tete*, or grandfather on my father's side, who used a thumb-mark with an ink cross to draw his pension, sent me to kindergarten for the purpose of learning Russian. He dreamt of the day when I would study in *Maskeu* (Moscow). Through rain, hail and snow, he would carry me on his back across the city. There was one funny incident when we were living temporarily in a mud house whilst my father erected our new house. Pacing back and forth, I prattled away to myself, believing that I was speaking Russian.

Tete was sixty years old by the time his eldest son, my father, returned safely from the war and produced a child. According to the Kazakh tradition, all firstborns are sent off to be brought up by their paternal grandparents.

I was adored by my elderly relatives! Before I was old enough to go school, I slept in same bed as my grandparents, wedged between them. I then moved onto a folding bed in their room whilst my younger brother Bekaydar took my place in their bed. I was considered grandfather's "daughter", whilst Bekaydar became known as my grandmother' "son".

I was breastfed by my grandmother. It sounds incredible, but this fifty three year old woman actually managed to produce breast milk when she received the joyful news of the birth of the long-expected granddaughter. Meanwhile, my real parents adopted the roles of elder brother and sister and throughout my childhood I called my mother by her name: Layla. Copying me, the younger children also called mother, Layla. Deeply offended by this habit, *Ani*, our Tatar grandmother, used to tell them grudgingly: "If you won't call her mother, then at least use the Kazakh *Apa*."

At school, things became confused by my referring to my mother by her name and my Kazakh grandparents would not tolerate hearing me calling her Layla in their presence. Later on, a compromise was reached and we, her children, as well as all of our friends, addressed her as *Sheshe*: an appropriate term for a mother in Kazakh.

Father's parents were illiterate people and did not speak Russian. Nevertheless, they were very interested in my school life: what I was up to, my friends and what grades I obtained. There was a brief period when I could not express my thoughts properly since I was using the Russian language at school but then, using a combination of my two languages, I began relating to them in detail, everything that had happened during my day.

MZIYA, MARZIYA, MARUSYA...

Friends, whom I have found on the Internet, know me as Mziya. It is a kind of tribute to the memory of my grandparents. I was born in Aktyubinsk, while they lived in Temir, a small district town. When I was born, my parents sent a message to my grandparents asking them to suggest a girl's name.

My Grandfather's daughters, my aunts and my father's younger sisters, were called Ayniya and Zaniya so they decided to give me a name Mziya. My parents couldn't understand it since they had never heard of such name so when they registered my birth, I was named Marziya on the birth certificate. Mziya is in fact, a real name, very popular in the Caucasus. Whenever my grandparents communicated with me they addressed me as Mziya, Mzan or Mzeken, but my father called me Mzushka.

I became known as Marusya in kindergarten. On the way to the kindergarten for the first time, I was instructed by mother: "Do not call yourself by your real name Mziya. Instead, you may tell them that your name is Marziya". A nursery teacher, Tamara Viktorovna, declared to the children gathering around me: "We have a newcomer. What is your name?" Being very quiet and timid I could barely whisper: "Marziya". The nursery governess asked me: "Can you repeat that, please?" When I was too shy to answer, she announced: "Okay: we'll call you Marusya" and that is how I became known as such.

Later on, when our kindergarten group started school, I continued to be called Marusya. However, when I reached adolescence, I became embarrassed by that name. I now realize that the name itself sounds quite pretty and delicate but at that time, "Marusya" conjured up in my mind, the image of a strong and busty hussy with spade-like arms and so in upper school, I arranged to be called Mariya or Marina. It wasn't until I presented myself as Marziya in the first year of University, that I was known by my real name but some of my friends in Temir still call me Marusya.

SOME WORDS ABOUT THE FORMATION
OF MY CHARACTER

When I was growing up, I behaved like a reckless boy. I hated and still dislike wearing headscarves and when I was young, usually dressed in a cap with ear-flaps, trousers and vest. My evenings were spent gathering in our flock of sheep, making and rolling out the dough for the meat to be cooked according to a Kazakh recipe (the only dish accepted by my grandfather) and milking the cow whilst trying to ignore the boys whistling for me to join their games. I sometimes managed to persuade my younger sister Naziya to milk the cow and if I hadn't already prepared the dough, would ask her to do that for me as well, so that I could run off down the street to play.

Once when I was carrying on with the boys, I turned my ankle and broke my leg but afraid that they would forbid me from joining in the boys' games in the future, I told my parents that I slipped and fallen on the ice which had formed around a downpipe. I also broke my arm when learning to skate and used to ski, play volleyball, hockey and football. I won first place in the regional chess competition, a great event of that period, and so in general, I was a keen sportswoman and socially active person. To tell the truth, I don't rate my looks but my husband describes me as a pretty woman. He repeats this sentiment so often that I used to suspect that he was having me on!

Gathering beside the Temir River on the outskirts of the city was one of the local children's a favourite pastimes and several of the areas which had been cleared of vegetation even had their own names: Plotina,

Malchishye, Bolnichnaya and Tekhnikum. Once I had a bet with the boys to see which one of us could swim to Tekhnikum, a distance of almost three or four kilometres.

We were to start by swimming from the deep waters of Malchishye all the way to the shallow waters of Tekhnikum. The whole of the area was covered with reeds and the so-called *kushars*; rigid troublesome slime ascending from the riverbed. And so it was that three boys and I commenced this dangerous swimming "bet" at two o'clock in the afternoon. Although the river looked harmless, there were also a lot of violent whirlpools in the Temir which coupled with the slime, had claimed the lives of many people. We were therefore accompanied, as a precaution, by a one oared boat. As we progressed, one of the boys developed a nosebleed and then the others felt too short of breath to continue. And so I was abandoned, all alone, half-way between Bolnichnaya and Tekhnikum.

It was a scary and difficult experience; I was especially frightened of the kushars which scratched at your body as if they were alive, but I would not stop and give up the bet. As a result, I did my best to reach the shore. With gritted teeth; I continued swimming against the current …

I reached the Tekhnikum shallows by six o'clock. Tottering, I emerged from the water to discover that even the hairs on my skin were matted with slime. I had a quick swim in clean water and then, with legs as stiff as boards, slowly started for home. Remonstrated with questions about where I had been, the terrors of my four hour swimming ordeal dissolved from my mind and I hurried off to gather in the sheep.

This dangerous adventure was one of the first tests in my life which taught me to overcome obstacles, whatever the circumstances. The memory of this event and the feeling of victory have remained with me since childhood and there were to be many more experiences in my life which had the same impact.

There is however, another side to the coin.

With the passing of years, people began to think that I was made of steel instead of being an ordinary human being: According to them, I had powers akin to a "Terminator". Sometimes I feel very upset when I hear people talking about how strong I am and how little it surprises them that I am able to withstand conditions which others would find impossible. I would much prefer to be recognized for my gentle nature and for people to acknowledge that I am actually as sensitive as everyone else despite my hard exterior.

I must confess that I grow tired of the unlimited faith which people around me seem to place in my powers and there are times when I begin to think that I have become far too disconnected from my more vulnerable side in my continuous attempts to focus body and mind on fighting adversity. I cannot allow myself to be defeated by anything or anyone and live according to my principles, but please believe me when I tell you that it is far from easy and requires a lot of effort.

CHILDHOOD

My siblings and I were much loved but were never indulged: as was the common practice of all large families during that era, children were expected from an early age to take responsibility for various and often arduous domestic duties including housework and gardening.

The climate is very arid in the area where I grew up and since the water pump was located two kilometres from the house, collecting water was an arduous chore. In addition, since the water ran deep, it often remained out of reach. When I was in fifth form, it was my job to harness the horse to a cart or sledge and collect our water in a large barrel.

Fuel for the furnace was prepared from natural sources and we used a sharp knife to cut out sections of sheep or cow dung which had become hard-pressed in layers on the ground. Once day, when I riding bareback to gather winter fuel, the horse took fright and bolted. As he galloped at full speed into the sand covered square near the bazaar, I decided to jump off and closing my eyes, leapt from his back. I was very lucky that I didn't break anything and thereafter, always used tack when riding that same horse!

Another of my jobs was to join the adults in piling sacks of potatoes onto my shoulders and then heaving them onto the back of a truck. Our potatoes, which were sold to neighbouring areas, provided money to buy hay since this was scarce in Aktyubinsk.

If my younger sisters dawdled over their chores or ignored my instructions, it was I, as the eldest who got into trouble and on one occasion, when I hadn't done the dishes after dinner, my mother met me at the door with a dirty saucepan in her hands and then proceeded to chase me around the house beating me with the broom!

By narrating aspects of my childhood, it is my aim to illustrate influences which impacted upon the development of my character. I studied hard and with pleasure, but I had to do my homework on the run since there was much which demanded my attention outside school: in addition to housework, there were events connected to literary societies and sports and being a great book lover, I found that the only time left for reading, was night time.

MY DEAR GRANDPARENTS

From childhood, I helped my grandpa with the haymaking and during the harvest; my grandparents always went to gather the spicula which had been left behind by the combines. Grandpa had a Kurke – a type of the tilt cart as big as a wagon and covered with a canvas cloth – and when they went to the steppe, this is where we lived for a week or two.

Once they went without me. They worked long and hard all day long gathering the spicula which then had to be threshed, winnowed and poured into sacks. According to my grandmother, my grandfather, who was a man of unbending spirit, suddenly began to cry during supper. "What's wrong with you, old man?" asked my startled grandma. "What if Mzeken is feeling upset or doesn't have enough food?" replied grandpa and without finishing his food, he saddled a horse and galloped the ten kilometres home. He then quickly collected my things and seating me in front of him, rode back to my grandma.

Although illiterate, my elderly relatives were nevertheless eager to gain knowledge. They were restrained in their spending but never skimped on books and amassed such a large library that our neighbours used to regard their house as the village reading room.

When he received his pension, my grandfather who was unable to read or write, became a regular customer at the cultural goods shop and the bookstore where he purchased historical works and publications of Kazakh epics. He also bought records because he adored listening to songs by Garifulla Kurmangaliev and the kyui (folk singer) Kurmangazi. Whenever they were on the radio, we children would run outside to where the grown-ups were engaged in farming activities, and shout: "*Tete* (grandfather), *Meme* (grandmother), Garifulla is singing!" My grandparents would then immediately down tools and rush home to listen to the music!

At home, the whole family used to enjoy literary evenings and with his children at his side, Dad would read through the great epics one after another.

In tribute to the memories of my grandparents, tete and meme, I have always taught both my children and grandchildren, the importance of being true to oneself and regardless of what obstacles may fall in your path, you must always strive to do your best or not do anything at all, especially if there is a risk of compromising other people. My elderly relatives were always prepared to get their hands dirty and in reward for their personal integrity, sensitivity and high regard for intellectual culture, commanded respect from all who knew them. Even the most desperate hooligans would temper their behaviour when encountering my serious and laconic grandfather.

Ani, my grandmother on my mother's side, also contributed much to my upbringing. In 1942 her husband was killed in the war and at the age of just thirty seven, she was left alone with five young children.

Being a strong-willed and hard-working woman, Ani taught me from an early age how to care for the vegetable garden and to keep an assiduously clean house. The plot of land where she grew her vegetables was five kilometres from the city of Temir, in the Aktyubinsk Region where our family then lived. We sometimes travelled by horse and cart but more often than not, Ani and I went by foot.

Some words about my mother

Layla, Sheshe, Meme... I remember her as a hard-working mother who loved and was devoted to her children. I was regarded as the daughter of my grandparents, tete and meme and after they died, Sheshe revealed that they had prohibited her from not only hugging and kissing me but also from treating me favourably. The elders had been prone to jealousy and even if in conversation, I unintentionally made reference to being my mother's daughter, they perceived this as an act of betrayal. That was why for a long time; I called my mother by her name, Layla or Laylyushka.

Sheshe, as we all eventually called her, was my best female friend and confidante throughout my childhood. She took an interest in everything I did and whenever I returned from parties, she would ask me and I would tell her all about my male admirers. I could talk to her about anything and she was always there to settle any problem. I now try to pass on to my own children, the feelings of confidence which Sheshe invested in me. I have never forced my ideas or tastes upon my son or daughter and have tried not to influence their life choices, preferring to simply offer guiding comments to prevent them from making mistakes.

After the death of my father, things changed and instead of Sheshe looking after me, our roles were reversed and she would often come to me for advice. She was a very positive and cheerful person, despite her hardships. It had not been easy for her to immediately integrate with her husband's family since her Kazakh in-laws made high demands of their *kelin* or daughter-in-law, not least because she was of a different nationality. My father's parents were severe by nature but she managed to earn their love and respect and she too, became strict with her own children. If ever we did anything wrong, my tete and meme would threaten to tell Layla and seeing our mother's puckered brows, we would know that we were in for a punishment!

I am very grateful to my mother for her maternal self-sacrifice. As soon as she heard about the accident and my injuries, she travelled by various means of transport to arrive in Ust Kamenogorsk that very night and stayed with me for a whole year. I was a terrible patient and my behaviour towards her, made worse by medication, was cruel and shameful. Upset by my shouting and blaming her for everything, the poor woman would retreat to the kitchen and burst out crying but then return with food for me. She was an elderly woman of sixty five yet indulged my every need and mood swing as though I were a small child. After a year, I regained my senses but even today, I still feel ashamed of the way I treated her.

I wonder whether my dear Sheshe can hear my tardy repentance. She died last December but I nevertheless want to thank her for her patience and her great maternal love towards me. Today I am known as a paragon of a wife and mother and an excellent housewife. Everything I know I have learnt from her. The essential characteristics I have inherited from my mother are to be tolerable and tolerant. My Dad was far from perfect and used to drink and use bad language but in spite of this she loved him heartily, never dwelling on his bad deeds and praising the good ones. He reciprocated her feelings. I once taunted him by asking: "Dad, do you love Sheshe?" My father looked confused, then mumbled something and turned to hug Mum with tears in his eyes. No words were needed as an answer.

Sheshe remained lively and young in spirit right up until the day she died and my daughter has fond memories of her exclaiming: " Okay: Let's go girls!"

My heart feels like it is breaking when I think about my mother. Let Sheshe forgive me, but I restrain myself from grieving for her because that would affect my sense of well-being. Although the anniversary of Sheshe's death approaches, I long more than ever to go to Temir and call in for a chat. Rest in Peace, Sheshe: I do hope that you have been reunited with Dad in heaven but even if heaven doesn't exist, you will remain on earth through cherished and deep memories.

Some words about my father

My earliest memory of my father goes back to when I was four or five years old. He regularly attended courses in Alma-Ata and I used to rush out of the house to greet him whenever he came home. On this occasion Dad had brought me a box which he opened there and then on the street. Imagine my delight in discovering a doll and a wonderful set of child-size utensils including tiny cups, forks and spoons. Next time, father brought oranges, tangerines and lemons from his trip to the city and I remember my family gathering around the table to sample all of these fruits which could rarely be found in the countryside.

I enjoyed a happy and comfortable childhood, filled with far too many memories of events to describe here. One of the best however, was when my parents spent an entire night making me a snowflake costume and crown for New Year and it was so beautiful that when I came on stage at the matinee of the children's performance I was not a mere snowflake but a Queen!

Both father and mother were fond of reading and had a good source of books in the library accumulated by Sheshe and my illiterate grandfather. When we went to bed, Sheshe and Dad would sit avidly reading and nibbling sunflower seeds and then stay up late into the night discussing what they had read.

I have fond memories of the evenings of literature and music which took place in our house. We children would be in charge of turning the handle of the record player so that we could all listen to the kuyi Kurmangazy. Nowadays, when I'm going through a bad period, I find solace in kuyis or folk music, especially when the dombra is played. Daddy also loved to read aloud Kazakh legends, entertaining both the family and our neighbours and these stories lifted our souls and raised our awareness of the commonness of the objective reality.

My father has been a major guide in my life: He was a very fair and honest person who liked to call a spade a spade. Like him, I cannot stand lies and duplicity but at times this trait has caused trouble. Now history is repeating itself in my son Baurzhan who tells me: "You have taught me not to lie, but telling the truth and always speaking my mind can have serious repercussions".

I know very little about what my father did in the war since he disliked talking about it. "Why do you want to know? War is terrible!" He always looked forward to Victory Day holiday, which fell on the 9th of May and much enjoyed drinking the 100g of alcohol dedicated by the People's Commissariat. As a young girl, this would cause me to argue: "You are the communist and you mustn't drink. I am a young member of the Communist Party: What kind of example are you setting for me?" The father would simply reply: "My dear Mzushka, forgive me!"

My Daddy loved me very much not least because he recognized some of his own characteristics in me and of all the children, I looked most like him.

I remember one more touching episode from my childhood. I was about five years when Dad bought me skates, bound to valenki (felt boots) with thongs. He taught me to skate and I continued to use these skates until I replaced them when I became a student. I learned how to master intricate movements to music and felt triumphant as I glided across the ice!

What else can I say about my unforgettable parents? We had a great family and we the children of Layla and Nurtaza, hold our heads high, proud to be Aukhinovs.

DAD'S DIARY FROM THE FRONT-LINE

Being a maximalist in my convictions, I have always responded critically to matters related to betrayal and decency. I take after my father: an honest man who lived by his principles. He could not and did not, want to act against his conscience.

It is notable that he kept a diary during the war. After he had returned home, it was presumed lost and he suspected that it had been accidentally burned by Sheshe or meme when they lit the fire under the cauldron containing *Tary*, a Kazakh national dish made from millet. The diary, which was discovered after his death, contained a candid account of his experiences. When excerpts from this courageous heart-felt journal were later published, the editor of one newspaper review saw fit to pen the heading: "Where are you, Warrior of Temir?"

But why were we so convinced that this precious diary had been burnt? It was always hard to find firewood on the drought affected steppe and so to fuel the furnace, we used anything that came to hand, including pressed dung, grass, old newspapers and exercise books.

It takes a long time to boil and simmer Tary in a large cauldron. Care must be taken to ensure that it doesn't become too soft. When ready, the dish is spread over special wooden boards to dry and then refried in the same cauldron and stirred with a special wooden paddle.

The preparation of Taty-Talkan is a real hassle but well worth the effort since it is both delicious and versatile: it is added to tea, eaten with milk or blended with sour cream and butter. Traditionally and especially in our region, it was never eaten with biscuits although this is now quite common. These days, Talkan made from millet is a delicacy, but during my childhood, this was an everyday dish.

So, returning to Dad's front-line diary. You may be wondering how it came to be discovered after his death. A journalist has described how he came across it when he was sorting through the archives of his own father, who was also a journalist. When Dad's youngest brother Sultan was demobilized, he immediately went to the editorial office in Kandagach and the diary was safely returned home. Kairat is planning to publish these front-line records in the form of a separate book for our grandchildren and great-grandchildren.

After the war, my father worked as a militiaman but following a serious incident, resigned. He disliked his new work as a foreman at the Road Department and in my opinion; stress was a large factor in his contraction of the disease which caused his early death. Up until the end of his life he regretted being forced to leave the militia: it was a clearly a case of unfair treatment and nepotism or what today, would be openly termed corruption

SUYUNSHI, GOOD NEWS NURTAZA: YOUR NAYMANCHUK HAS ARRIVED!

The only two grandchildren who my father managed to see before he died were my Baurzhan, or Naymanchuk, as my father tenderly called him, and Argyn, my brother Bekaydar's son. Until he was four, Baurzhan was brought up by my parents. Kairat and I desperately wanted our son to be with us but it was impossible since we had yet to find a permanent home.

I had difficult delivery with my first baby and also suffered from severe mastitis. I gave birth at the district hospital to which I had been transferred after becoming ill at the maternity hospital. According to the women in the ward, I suddenly lost consciousness and turned blue as a result of an allergic reaction to one of the drugs. They felt sorry for tiny Baurzhan: Who would take care of him? In spite of everything I survived, thanks to my *Aruakhs*, the spirits of my forefathers.

At our request, my grandmother and mother brought our son to Alma-Ata for the first time when he was two years old. When they were leaving, my grandmother asked: "How are you going to look after this child if you are working and Kairat is studying in Novosibirsk?" "We'll see", I mumbled "Perhaps we'll get a babysitter." "And how can you afford that?" she retorted. It was a reasonable question. We had no money to spare: Kairat was a post-graduate student and since I had newly qualified, I was still on a minimum wage.

They sat for a while and then announced their decision: "There's no way, my dear that you will be able to cope: we won't leave the child with you".

We couldn't argue, even though we had insisted on them bringing our son to us. Of course, we had tried to find a solution and had planned to raise money and then bribe someone to obtain a place for our child in

---

Suyunshi –Anyone who has learned about the birth of a child, especially if it was a son ... sort of a hurry first notify relatives shouted suyunshi (news)

the day nursery…

Finally, my mother and grandmother took him away with them, which was fortunate given the repercussions at my parents' home. My father was already very unwell but continued working and had been away on a business trip when Baurzhan was taken to Alma-Ata. When he discovered the absence of his grandson, he flew into a rage and using bad language, threatened to kick his wife out of the house until the boy was returned.

Sheshe and Ani, with Baurzhan in her arms, arrived by air from Aktyubinsk and hailed down a passing car to take them the distance to my parents' house outside Temir city. Hearing a knock at the gates, the youngest brother Sultan ran out and seeing a feeding bottle protruding from one of the bags, ran off, shouting cheerfully: "Daddy, Baurzhan has come home!"

According to Kazakh tradition it is assumed that a child will be left with the father's parents, but in our case, my parents turned out to be more liberal. I didn't even ask: I simply took my son to them. Their lives were not easy: both were working and they were also caring for my elderly grandmother, but nevertheless, they accepted responsibility for the little baby and brought up Baurzhan until he was four years old.

Once our son was living with us, my Dad, who was by then very ill, eagerly awaited every visit. One day when we arrived home, men living nearby made my father very happy by announcing: "Nurtaza, suyunshi (good news), your naymanchuk has arrived". Dad, so overjoyed by the prospect of spending time with his grandson, gave them his entire week's pension!

My son was much loved in Temir city. When Kairat tried to correct Baurzhan by gently slightly slapping him for childish pranks, my grandmother, who rarely quarreled with her relatives, got so angry with him that she used to shout: "May your hands drop off!"

Both I and my little sisters, who enrolled in KazGU (the Kazakh

State University) after me, had a habit of coming home unexpectedly. My grandfather was always the first person we saw as we descended from the plane and as soon as term had ended he would visit the airport daily, whatever the weather, telling everyone: "Mzeken is coming home".

Later, my Dad adopted a similar role and when were no longer any planes to Temir and we were due to arrive for a holiday with little Baurzhan, he would go to the bus stop and wait for every bus. Anyone who saw him would know that Nureke was waiting for his grandchild and if someone saw Baurzhan coming off the bus before Dad, they would run up to my father cheerfully shouting: "Suyunshi (good news), your naymanchuk has arrived!"

THE BEST KELIN (DAUGHTER-IN-LAW) IN THE DISTRICT OF SAMARA

Kairat Zakiryanov

Although we share many points of view, my wife has the distinguishing capacity to believe that the whole world is light and pure. Is it because she is poetic by nature? To me it's an alien concept and there are times when I've told her: "I'm fed up with your poetic attitude".

She can be completely intolerant of anyone who behaves badly or has bad intentions and will break off her relationship with them and forget them altogether. Even if she has been friends with someone and they let her down, she will have no hesitation in cutting them loose. I used to reason and argue with her that when this was applied to mutual friends and colleagues, this placed us both in an uncomfortable position but she would still categorically refuse to accept their behavior.

About five years ago, when Marziya was again in hospital, she was visited by the elder brother of the mathematician Mukhtar Kitapbaev,

126

under whom she had worked at the Road Building Institute. Noshay Kitapbaev was a Hero of the Socialist Labor Party and despite it being rest hour when the ward was closed to visitors; he decided to burst in regardless.

The day before his visit, there had been celebrations to mark the 100th anniversary of the Samara District in the East Kazakhstan Region where I was born. There had been a ceremony in which special medals were presented to the most established and worthy natives of the district and I believe I had been named as a candidate. However, Boshat Kitapbaevich told me: "Kairat, it goes without saying that we are proud of you, but your wife is also worthy of a medal due to the good example she has set for all daughters-in-law in the district." He had personally overseen the production of both the certificate and the medal on which were inscribed: "To the Best Kelin of the Samara District".

Until that day, the *Aqsaqal* or respected Elder, had never met Marziya, but heard all about her from his younger brother Mukhtar. In order to congratulate her, this elderly person, with prosthesis had to walk up four flights of stairs.

...In the year, when we had just decided to become a family, I was working with the building brigade in the Kurtinsk District of Alma-Ata while Marziya remained in the city along with her younger sister who had enrolled at KazGU. Every three or four weeks, I had the opportunity to come into the city and used to travel by lorry in order to uplift building materials. As soon as I could, I would rush to meet her. We were once sitting embracing one another in the cab of the lorry when I realized that I wanted nothing else in life apart from being in the presence of this green-eyed girl dressed in a calico dress.

Our love has withstood many challenges: the lack of a permanent home, a lack of money, the birth and rearing of our children and I believe that through our experience of even greater and more severe obstacles, our family has become so strong that it is now indestructible.

Nowadays, many people get married without really discussing common goals or a lasting commitment and two years down the line, as the memories of their splendid wedding ceremony fade, the newlyweds realize that they can't stand each other. I've often wondered why it is that in the West; young people date for a long time and then live as a common-law couple before deciding to get married. Perhaps this is to ensure that no-one gets hurt in the future. Is this the way forward? Any married relationship is hard to break if based on love and attention to minor everyday details.

When I think about events which occurred ten or fifteen years ago, I must confess that I had no qualms about staying away overnight or going off on hunting trips for several days even though I knew that my wife was suffering at home. Had I known that each time I was away, I was probably shortening my beloved wife's life by up to one month; I would certainly have curbed my behaviour and relinquished such pleasures. However, what's done is done and there is nothing I can do to change the past.

BE SUBTLE IN YOUR PERSUASION

We decided not to borrow money from our parents for our wedding and in any case, Kairat's relatives had none to spare. I was however, offended by the fact that they took no interest at all in any of the preparations for their son's marriage. I simply couldn't understand it.

As for me, I was brought up in a very traditional family and it was the norm for matchmakers to call on the house to request permission to offer my hand in marriage. Knowing that I would not be following this part of our custom, I wrote a letter declaring that I was going to get married. My parents were silent and neither called nor wrote to me. I therefore wrote a second letter informing them that we had planned to file an application to the Civil Registry Office on a particular date and still, they remained silent. I then booked a long-distance call and found only my elderly grandmother and oldest brother at home. Since my grandmother was hard of hearing, I could only speak to my brother but he refused to answer any of my questions and repeated just one phrase: "I don't know and Dad is at work".

It turned out that my mother had had a stroke and had been admitted to hospital but my relatives had decided not to tell me since they knew how upset I would feel. My father was confused and grandma could not be given responsible for my destiny. They did not know how to respond to my letters and I hadn't given them enough information for them to enlist help from the matchmakers. And so the problem remained unresolved.

We were eager to arrange the wedding ceremony for October, when the weather was warm, and because both sets of parents were remained uncooperative, Kairat decided take matters into his own hands. He had a special status in his family and his parents had pinned high hopes on him.

Skipping ahead for a moment, I remember one of the last moments of his mother's life. Addressing her children who were gathered around her bed, she told them: "Almaniya, as the elder, will remain the head of the family, but you must obey Kairat since he is the one who is capable of making decisions".

In the case of our wedding, he decided to approach my parents while adopting the role of a matchmaker, taking the serious risk of being refused my hand. I had no alternative but to send them a telegram worded: "Please, answer me: Will you bless our marriage or not?!"

At last there came the short reply we had been waiting for: "We'll bless you".

In all of the wedding pictures, my mother's face appears slightly askew as a consequence of her stroke. As I later told relatives attending our wedding, my mother wasted no time in contacting me as soon as she had been discharged from hospital. On arrival in Temir, 250 kilometres from Aktyubinsk, she immediately called to ask me which items from my "bottom drawer", I would like her to bring to the wedding. During her lifetime my mother purchased four of everything: One was meant for her own household use and the other three were put aside for her daughters. I told her that as we planned to rent temporary accommodation, we would only need the bare necessities.

From my side, my father, mother and Ani were present at the wedding. They stayed with Kairat's relatives on his mother's side. In the summer time, when I was home for the holidays, I noticed a pair of splendid men's shoes for fifty five roubles at the shoe shop where my mother worked and asked her to save them for me. Not only did she bring the shoes, but she also purchased a beautiful shirt for her future son-in-law. In addition, she also brought along a cut glass vase which I had acquired when cutting the first sod for a project undertaken by the building brigade.

Mother began distributing her presents: platform shoes and a shirt for Kairat and dress patterns for his female relatives... Taking me aside, Kairat whispered: "Don't be surprised if my relatives haven't bought any clothes for you". He was quite right; there were no gifts and only his sister-in-law Almaniya, in response to a prompt from Kairat, bothered to wander round the shops to pick up a blouse for me.

Kairat excuses his parents by explaining that there are no traditions in their region of giving presents to either the kelin or her relatives but had he insisted, they would have acted like matchmakers, bought gifts and invited my parents to their house.

In my opinion, the situation was quite different: His mother, responsible for eight children, had simply no time to indulge in the luxury of sentiment.

Her day began at five a.m. when she had to fire up the stove, knead dough, bake bread, get the children ready and then hurry with them along to the school where she worked as a teacher of Kazakh language and literature. Kairat's parents worked hard but they were always short of money and the children were forever wearing out their clothes and shoes. Kairat felt sorry for his parents but understanding the situation between them and me, refused to take sides.

Though my parents, with all their deference to the observation of tradition did not lay any blame on Kairat's parents for their apparent disinterest in them, I nevertheless teased Kairat by asking: How come I have no parents? Did I simply drop from the sky?! I wonder whether they will take the same attitude when their own daughters marry." As a result, we had fierce arguments on the subject…

He has recently begun to take heed of what I've been saying but more importantly, and in spite of his relatives' attitude towards me, I quietly performed all the household duties expected of a Kazakh kelin. We spent all of our holidays at his homeland where even though no one told me what to do, I worked tirelessly from morning till night: brushing up, washing, cleaning, cooking and visiting guests.

Let's return to the story of our wedding. All of our student friends joined in the celebrations and afterwards, accompanied us to our temporary housing on Papanin Street. The next day both sets of parents were expected to visit the newlyweds and no longer a bride but a wife, I decided to fry eggs for my husband's breakfast prior to their arrival. I didn't have a frying pan so instead, used an aluminum saucepan, and this is how we shared our first meal as a family.

Fortunately, we were well prepared and our guests were entertained ceremoniously and honorably. One of Kairat's female relatives couldn't resist lifting the corner of the blanket on our bed and when I noticed a happy look on her face, I knew that she was satisfied by what she had seen.

Afterwards, Sheshe and father returned home, but Ani, my Tatar grandmother, decided to stay for a while on the pretext of searching for a coat. In all likelihood her main reason for staying had more to do with exerting control over how we would run our home!

Before she left, I had a chance to ask my mother for the real reason behind the family's silence when I had announced my intention to marry, and told her that had they said "No!" to the union, I would never have disobeyed them.

Mother said nothing and I later realized that my parents would have been afraid to say "no" because they doubted my chastity and were worried that I might have been pregnant. However, their suspicions were groundless since my conscience was imbued with morals sewn by my grandfather and both Kazakh and Tatar grandmothers.

Premarital relations, particularly where girls were concerned, were highly disapproved of my by parents' families and although it was never discussed directly, we were in no doubt that such behaviour would bring shame on the family.

An exploration of chastity, virginity and romantic attitudes towards love was cultivated through literature where falling in love was described primarily, as the attraction between two souls. In all of my romantic relationships I was very impulsive, but premarital sex was strictly prohibited. It was accepted that this should be saved for the wedding night.

Recently, I had a conversation with my daughter regarding to this delicate matter. I asked Asel whether she had had premarital relationships with Mars, her husband. To my great pleasure, my daughter answered: "You always told me to retain my innocence and by virtue of this, our family relationship would be strong. Mars respected me for this and I in turn, shall bring up my daughter in the same manner".

Of course, the person with whom you fall in love, may go off and look for someone with different moral values but that will be his or her problem. If someone falls seriously in love with you and regards as you as their destiny, that means that they must respect your principles. If instead, he or she turns around and looks for someone else then you have been saved from spending the rest of your life with someone who is fickle

and unreliable. You and your honour are worth more than that…
I don't pretend to know what the ideal family looks like and can only base my ideas on the foundation of this kind of "social unit" by referencing my own. Speaking candidly, I made several attempts to break up with Kairat after we had quarreled but faced with my threats he would always respond: "Whatever happens, I will come to you!" and if I replied: "I won't open the door" he would simply tell me that he would climb in the window! Of course, despite our heated debates and arguments it was never really my intention to get divorced. We were intimately and spiritually bound to each other by a thin yet stable thread: something which I recognized from the very beginning but which I suspect Kairat didn't appreciate until a little later...

MY FATHER DIES IN MARZIYA'S ARMS

Kairat Zakiryanov

We never had any money to spare at home even though my father held the position of Department Manager at the state farm, and my mother worked as a teacher. I remember the delight in my mother's eyes when I brought home one thousand roubles which I'd earned with the building brigade: she had never before held such a great sum of money in her hands.
Aware of their financial position, I did not ask my parents for money when I decided to get married
Money for the wedding was earned from my work with the building brigade and with some help from my fellow students; I hired the "Alma-Ata" restaurant, the height of luxury in 1975. The wedding ceremony took place on the 6th floor and was attended by eighty guests.
Through our own efforts we also purchased Marziya's wedding dress

and veil as well as the wedding rings and my suit. However, these actions did not sit well with Marziya's traditional Kazakh upbringing even though I as a Shala-Kazakh or "Kerzhak" from East Kazakhstan did not observe the same customs.

I tried to assure her that my parents were open-hearted and kindhearted people in spite of their apparent severity, but she would not listen: Marziya was offended because they had not followed the matchmaking tradition. Had she told me beforehand how important this was to her, I would gladly have asked my parents to act accordingly but being used to so-called "Komsomol Weddings", devoid of any traditional ceremonies, my relatives simply assumed that they could get acquainted with her family at the wedding.

I was angry about by my wife's indifferent attitude towards my relatives and we often quarreled about this but when my parents, first my mother and then my father became sick, Marziya demonstrated the best aspects of her character: kindness and tenderness. When she went to take care of my mother after a major operation, my aunt Raufa-apai held her up as an example to everybody, even my sisters who had no intention to leaving their jobs for the sake of my mother.

When father was pronounced terminally ill, he did not want people in his community to see how he had been reduced from being a proud-spirited man to someone so feeble and dependent so he decided to spend his remaining days with his children in the city and then have his remains returned to his native village. Without beating around the bush, he announced: "I plan to spend one week at Almaniya's, the next at Marat's, the third at Kairat's, and my final week at Talgat's…"

However, by the end of his third day with us, he decided that he did not want to go anywhere else and as testimony of how dear she had become to my family, he declared: "I want to die in Marziya's arms."

Marziya's relationship with my brothers had also been strained. Like Marziya, my younger brother Talgat was also very forthright and as a result of an argument they didn't communicate for three years. However, as soon as he and Kanat, another of my brothers became aware of father's final diagnosis, they immediately called Marziya to apologize and make up.

Marziya knows how much her attitude towards my relatives hurts me but given the two parties' often conflicting points of view and her refusal to compromise her beliefs and adopt a gentler, softer approach, I just have to accept the fact that my beloved wife and relatives will forever find offence in their differences..

It's simply a fact of life that she lives according to her philosophy but equally to her warm and generous nature.

SHE SWALLOWED HER TEARS, SUBJECTED TO ALL THIS, PRETENDING SHE WAS FINE

I have been known for being very forthright since childhood and have inherited this characteristic from my grandfather and father. For the most part, my husband's relatives cannot stand it and occasionally criticize me. My now deceased mother-in-law found it hard to take me to her bosom and similarly, Kairat's siblings did not warm to me. Whenever there arose any discord between me and his family, I immediately informed Kairat who naturally, found it tiresome.

In contrast to my relationship with other members of my new family, I always got on well with my father-in-law. He was a wise and honorable man, who in common with my own father, was a dedicated communist .Unlike his wife who selfishly loved only her own children, he respected and loved me. Everything appeared to be fine on the surface but I was eager to understand what lay in their hearts and souls since I disliked any superficiality. It was completely the opposite situation in my family where we all had an open understanding of each other. When my father married my mother, she already had a baby but nevertheless, my grandparents accepted her as their own daughter, even though after the war, there were plenty of other young, single girls. In the documentary film about our family, my mother confessed that at death's door my grandfather kissed her hands saying: "Aynalayin, rakhmet. Men sagan rizamyn", meaning: "I am satisfied with you, and die without any hard feelings towards you".

Kairat's mother was a good person who was devoted to her eight children but having always felt like an outsider, I wanted to prove through my relationship with Svetlana, my son's wife, that it is possible to build a warm and close relationship with the young woman who was entering our family. We lived under the same roof for eleven years and regardless of the fact that she had a different cultural background and upbringing, we never quarreled. Through this experience, I sadly realize how much better the relationship could have been between Kairat's mother and me.

EXTENDING OUR LINEAGE

There was one further consequence of my mother-in-laws' refusal to follow wedding traditions. Kairat was away at military training on the day I was due to give birth to our son so during the month before my delivery, I was all alone in Alma-Ata. I could not return home because his parents had never visited my parents, my husband was absent and I was pregnant. No -one apart from my father, mother and grandmother had attended the wedding so what would my neighbours have thought if they had seen that I was pregnant?

With nowhere else to go, I had no option but to travel to the distant state farm in the region of East Kazakhstan where the husband's parents lived. I arrived on July 18th. On the way I purchased a few necessary items for the new baby: little loose jackets, bootees and a piece of flannel for swaddling. It was considered bad luck to buy baby things before the child had been born but I knew that I would be unable to get even the basics in the village.

My husband's paternal home was far from clean and tidy and without even having a cup of tea, I began to put things in order. Too late, but anticipating my arrival and reaction to the state of the house, Kairat's younger brother Kanat had rushed home to try to clean things up. My due date was estimated as August 17th and it had been my intention to leave on the first of the month for Ust Kamenogorsk. However, this was not to be. My first task was to freshen up the room which I had been given and this involved whitewashing the walls, painting the floors and windows, boiling clothes and hanging blinds. Once I'd finished and finding it hard to sit around doing nothing, I moved on to the next room and carried on until I had cleaned and decorated the entire house.

I then decided to render and whitewash the exterior walls. After I had mixed the mortar, Kairat's younger brothers assisted me by dragging the buckets to the wall. I had hardly climbed the ladder when I realized that I needed more mortar and called for the boys. Since they had scampered off to play, I had no choice but to get it myself but as I grasped hold of a heavy bucket, I felt an internal tremor, as if something had torn...

In between rendering the walls, I also did all the cooking: no small undertaking since in the summer there could be as many as thirty people gathered at Kairat's parents' house, including his brothers, their wives and children and other relatives. Everyone was desperate to escape the awful smog of Ust Kamenogorsk. As a result, meals were served in three shifts and prepared in canteen-sized saucepans.

Through force of habit, I took charge of everything, including the kitchen: I was neither asked nor forced to do this but I believed it to be my duty as the *kelin* or daughter-in-law.

Earlier that year , we had brought a KamAZ (lorry) filled with facing bricks for Kairat's late father's mazar and descending from the cab in an elegant crepe-de-chine dress, I immediately set about helping the children to unload and stack the bricks. Meanwhile, the adults were waiting to be served their tea and I caught a glimpse of my mother-in-law nodding her head: whether she was condemning or praising my actions, is anyone's guess but I've no doubt that she was talking about my inability to sit still. I later learned that it is believed that the evil eye is responsible for behavior deemed to be over-active and restless!

I often wonder why I like Tamoska's poems. Even though they are not perfect, the feelings described in the poetry strikes a chord within me. Kairat cannot feel it but I suspect that one of my grandchildren will come to empathize with his work.

Just once, even with experience and effort,
Not everyone may straighten his spinal cord.

Or:

...She swallowed her tears,
Subjected to all this,
Pretending she was fine.

This is a description of me: There has been so much pain and despair, hardships and difficulties against which I did not react or complain about!

But I have again strayed from events related to the birth of my boy. Well, I needed the mortar and with little time to complete the work, and nobody around to help, I lifted the bucket myself. By then it was almost three o'clock, lunchtime, and I had to feed everyone...

Masha, my brother-in-law Marat's wife, fed the youngest first and then those who were students and senior pupils sat down to eat. Afterwards there was tea to be served but even before Masha had appeared with a large white kettle, I realized that I was standing in a puddle of water and worse, it was still pouring out of me every time I moved!

When Masha asked "Marziya, serve the tea, please", I suggested that she do it instead but she insisted: "No, you manage this better than me". Embarrassed, I had no idea how I could move away from the table since I was surrounded not only by boys but by young men. Fortunately, the entrance to the kitchen was covered with a fly-net, and I was able to pull it across me to conceal my wet dress as I sat dripping in a cold sweat. Suddenly, hearing the gaggle of geese outside, I found a perfect excuse to escape! "Oh!" I exclaimed "I'd better go out and check that the children don't get pecked by the geese!" And with this, I rapidly headed for the exit of the makeshift dining area.

I ran to the house to change my dress but had not even had time to remove it before I felt the water running again. I honestly had no idea what was happening! My chaste family had not educated me on the subject of pregnancy and because I had had exams to sit at University, I had not attended any anti-natal classes. From the back of my mind however, came a vague memory of someone mentioning waters breaking just before childbirth…

Fortunately, the boys had left the kitchen, leaving only Masha. I leant against the doorpost and told her about what had happened. She turned pale and immediately sent her husband to call for Nursipat, the local doctor's assistant. Unfortunately, it transpired that she had gone to a neighbouring village to perform *Kudalyk*, the request for a girl's hand in marriage, and would be delayed. Meanwhile, Kairat's parents had taken the car to buy school uniforms for their younger children.

I waited impatiently for Nursipat's bus to arrive. As soon as she got off, she recognized the urgency of my situation and ran off to hail down a car but since during harvest time petrol was scarce, none appeared. Eventually, she managed to stop a milk tanker which had only one litre of petrol but with me seated beside him in the cab, the driver rushed at full speed, taking a shortcut across bumpy tracks and fields. I met up with Kairat's parents at the hunters' lodge, on their way home: my mother-in-law had apparently predicted the day before that I would begin labour and had insisted that they return as quickly as possible. By the time I was transferred to my father-in-law's Moskvich, my body felt limp. We arrived at the maternity hospital at six o'clock and my baby was delivered at quarter to midnight.

The boy had no name for a month and in the meantime, while we awaited Kairat's return, he was known simply as Little One. I wanted to name him Rustem, but my mother-in-law insisted on Baurzhan. Kairat supported neither me nor his mother and since time was passing and we had to register the birth, I surrendered under pressure. At heart, I felt I deeply offended that I had not been allowed to choose my son's name, not least because no-one had displayed or acknowledged any sentiment of pity towards the difficult delivery.

It is worth mentioning that Kairat's mother had been allowed to choose names for each of her children! However, the name Baurzhan did no harm to anyone and had no influence on his destiny. As for me, I had my own ambitions as a young mother. I admit that I felt vexed that my husband did not support me in this matter but it was strange to see what fortune had in store: Kairat's sister Almaniya married late and her only son, named by her mother-in-law, was called Rustem!

ONE GOVERNMENT, MANY DIFFERENT PEOPLES

Kairat was never interested in genealogy before he met me: it was a subject in which his family took no interest. There are many Russians and Germans living in my husband's homeland, so the local Kazakhs became more *russified* than people living in other regions of Kazakhstan.

I remember early on in our relationship, when I was cooking in the students' hostel kitchen and Kairat was hanging around as usual trying to attract my attention, I suddenly asked him: "What clan are you from?" At first, he was a bit confused but then replied: "I am Shala–Kazakh". I burst out laughing: There is no such clan as Shala–Kazakh: the term refers to people who are not pure bred Kazakhs! To me it was a serious issue and so I recommended that he asked his eighty year old grandpa about his heritage and more importantly, which clan he belonged to.

I remember something else connected with this matter. I had enrolled to take an exam on the history of the Communist Party of the Soviet Union in which I had to address: "The Issue of Inter-Ethnic Relations in the USSR". It was beyond my comprehension why people would neglect and be required to ignore their languages and customs in order to be part of a unified nation. Confused, I answered the paper with clichés and as a result, I got only "Three" marks. This upset me greatly since I had prepared well for the exam and had never received such a low mark.

I still find it difficult to fathom the logic of Lenin's tracts and wonder how students who received high marks in exams related to inter-ethnic relations managed to do so without acting against their consciences. In the tragic December of 1986 I worked at the Ust Kamenogorsk Building-Road Institute. Kitapbaevich, Head of Department, and I were the only two Kazakhs amongst Russians. I also had many close friends who were Russian and it sent a shiver down my spine to think that any of these people nurtured an underlying, negative hostility towards Kazakhs.

God forbid that there is ever any major dispute concerning our national identity. I have always respected Nursultan Nazarbaev, the President of the Republic of Kazakhstan, especially during the first years of independence, for his ability to maintain amicable equality amongst the various ethnic groups which belong to our country.

In my opinion, it fundamentally wrong to hate a person on the basis of their nationality and different cultural background but an infra-structure needs to be put in place to educate people to think likewise. My mother was a Tatar from Kazan and my father was Kazakh. When we were children, our relatives used to joke about our mixed origins: my mother's family used to claim, ironically, that we were Kazakhs whilst my father's side placed more emphasis on our Tatar blood. The adults did not attach much importance to any of this but such comments left the children feeling uncomfortable and confused about their identity and hence, I always preferred to affiliate with my clan.

MY HUSBAND BELONGS TO THE SHAN CLAN

I am once again wandering away from the subject of the origins of Kairat's family tree. One day, having just returned from spending the holidays at home, he announced: "It turns out that I am from the Shan clan". I told him that there was no such clan among the large tribes since at that time, neither he nor I were aware of the appearance in 1700 B.C of nomads from the Shan clan who had been associated with the first imperial Yin dynasty in the Heavenly Empire. Kairat spent several of his holidays questioning his grandfather and discovered that primarily they had belonged to the Nayman clan, then the Matai clan (part of the Nayman Family), and finally, to the Karaulzhasak clan.

I breathed a sigh of relief as my dad had a dislike of members of the Tortqara clan (belonging to the Elimuly tribe), and I did not want to upset him. As for me, I decided to be friends with him since he belonged to the Shan clan. Today, this seems a rather peculiar stance to take but back then, it was the matter of importance for a girl from the patriarchal Kazakh family.

Later, when by coincidence my nephew and nieces all married into the Tortqara clan, my family couldn't have been happier!

These discussions with Kairat regarding his origins, cemented our early friendship. Under Soviet rule, we seriously believed that the survival of our heritage depended on a recognition and acceptance of our different clans and nationalities whether they be Kazakhs, Russians, Georgians, Armenians, etc.

ADAY WARRIOR WOMAN

From childhood, I have never been able to imagine what it would be like to be oblivious to my origins. For me, it would be akin to not knowing who your father, mother and grandparents were. In his excellent novel: "And Longer than a Century Lasts a Day", Chingiz Aytmatov created the "Mankurt", a person who has been forcibly deprived of memory. Fortunately, this has not happened to the Kazakh nation. My grandparents told me about my origins as soon as I was able to talk and understand such things: "You are from the Aday clan amongst whom is the Munal clan and another sub-clan called Qosqulaq". I also received instruction about all of my relatives spanning seven generations, as was expected by our folk tradition.

So what does the Kazakh nation comprise? It is a union of various Turkic tribes and clans but if history had moved in a different direction, there would now be instead, a number of individual nations - Nayman, Aday, and Qypshaq – each with its own identity.

For over seventy years, people from fifteen nations living within the USSR, were known throughout the world as Russians and it is only recently that people from my country have been distinguished as Kazakhs.

I was born in the western part of the Republic where from times immemorial, lived the warring Aday tribe. My father married a Tatar and produced five children who between us have characteristics which illustrate our different ethnic origins. Me, my brother Sultan and to some extent, my sister Torym are Kazakhs by nature while Naziya and Bekaydar are spiritually closer to the Tatars.

I have never hidden the truth about being half Tatar but my grandfather insisted that we all adopted his own Kazakh national identity. I can't speak my mother's language despite attempts made by Ani, my strict Tatar grandmother. Finding it very difficult and forever mangling my pronunciation, I gave up (May the *Aruakh*, of my Ani forgive me) deciding: "Let it be so, I'll manage to do without Tatar. I am Kazakh by nature and will speak my native language.

TRUTH IS BORN OF DEBATE

Kairat has written and published several books on the history of the Kazakh nation. His historical research was undertaken during the period when he was fighting for the Sports and Tourism Academy or rather, its protection against an invasion of corruption.

We arrived from Ust Kamenogorsk as naive provincials with open minds. Prior to this, Kairat had completed his first degree and had gone on to complete a post graduate course in Novosibirsk city: both experiences had instilled in him pure ideals and a strong belief in justice.

In the course of his life, Kairat had never, experienced betrayal on a monumental scale. As we had advanced our professions, we didn't strive to set the world on fire but rather, took the approach that good and conscientious work will always be appreciated by both management and our colleagues. Things had always run smoothly for Kairat and it was only when he took up his post at the Academy that extraordinary events began to occur.

It was the normal practice in our family to share our concerns and so when Kairat told me about his problems at work, I was distressed for him. He had taken to heart, a series of his employees' betrayals and turning to drink had made him feel worse. I had to try and fix the problem and spent many a long day and night searching for a solution.

At that time I was reading a lot about the history of Kazakhstan and the Kazakh nation. We had only been able to begin studying our history properly since 1991 because it was only then that we were granted freedom of speech and full, rather than partial, access to literature and archival material.

I recall reading the Russian translation of the "Baluan Sholak" in fourth or fifth grade. It was a patriotic love story which gave a wonderful account of the Kazakh batyr's (hero's), victories. Once, when I was suffering from severe toothache and reading this book, I found myself sobbing aloud and didn't know whether this was due to my pain or in response to the batyr's destiny. When my grandmother asked me: "Have you fallen in love with the Baluan?" "Yes", I replied, swallowing my tears, "I have fallen in love and have toothache to boot!"

Since the first time I read this book, I have associated the image of the batyr not with Khajimukan but with Sholak. It was like the reversal of fortune: Kairat was managing the troubled Sports and Tourism Academy, while the Sports Palace named after Baluan Sholak was operating in a completely different and more positive manner.

My devotion to history commenced when I was living on the third floor of a block of flats in Alma-Ata's Almagul neighbourhood. At the summer cottage our spare time had been spent outside or going for walks but this wasn't really an option when we moved to the apartment and so we concentrated on reading instead.

I regularly recounted what I had just read to Kairat who in turn, would often question the accuracy of the historical data. These books triggered his interest from the perspective of a scientist and researcher and be began a serious study of the facts presented in order to find sources for a multitude of hypotheses and affirmations, whilst taking into account mythology and the natural tendency for laypeople to elaborate upon and praise their history. His devotion to History soon became as focused as it had once been to Mathematics. Wishing to share his findings, he decided to publish but even after his first articles had been printed, even his closest friends still regarded his new found interest as a mere whim.

By way of encouragement, I used to tell him: "Truth is born of debate: let anyone who disagrees with you, express a counter argument which we will then afford our due consideration."

I wonder what kind of person is prepared to accept just one, single account of history, without questioning its validity or even reading alternative views. Is the Communist Party to blame: Or the fact that for so long, we could only access history through Soviet schoolbooks? In a period when so much data was inaccessible and hidden in archives, where did the authors of these books gather their information? Moreover, few of the writers had the language skills to draw facts from original source material...

After presenting his book "Under the Wolf's Nest: A Turkic Rhapsody" in December 2012 to the Royal Geographical Society of Great Britain, Kairat was invited to deliver lectures at Cambridge University the following spring.

Well in advance of the event and feeling anxious, he told me: "If the dates coincide with your appointment for chemotherapy in Seoul, I won't go." But I was firm in my response: "Whatever happens, you must deliver your lecture: it's not every scientist who gets invited to speak at Cambridge University!"

Fortunately, he did not have to face this dilemma: the date fell on 8th March, International Women's Day and although we had always celebrated this together, it had no influence whatsoever on my husband's acceptance of an invitation to lecture at one of the world's most prestigious universities!

How could I be anything but proud of my husband?!

FROM MATHEMATICIAN TO HISTORIAN

Kairat Zakiryanov

Marziya has never read any of my books until they are finished but she supports and encourages me "to conquer new scientific peaks". I can provide many examples of great Mathematicians who have diverted their attentions to other sciences. The patriarch of science Karl Gauss used to say: "Mathematics is the Queen of all Sciences". If one knows well its principles and understands its logic, then he or she will deal easily with the Chemistry, Astronomy or...even History.

Mikhail Mikhaylovich Postnikov, Doctor of Physical-Mathematical Sciences and teacher of many of our greatest mathematicians used to say: "I acknowledge that history is written by specialists in this field but I want them to explain to me, as a layperson, the reasons why through the ages, evolution has developed in a particular direction. However, the fact is that none can answer this question and neither the historians from Kazakhstan or Russia have a true knowledge of their own country or its leaders. In the USSR period they simply quoted Marx and Engels to provide the basis of all arguments. When I was a postgraduate student, I was interested by lectures delivered by Professor Mukanov on the theories and psychology of the application of quotations. ..

With reference to the history of our ancestors, I go against the grain when dealing with traditional beliefs. When they have read my books, my offspring and their descendants may well decide to discard them as nonsense or alternatively, acknowledge that my thoughts have helped them to recognize that they belong to a great nomadic people.

When I presented my book "Under the Wolf's Nest: A Turkic Rhapsody" at the Royal Geographical Society, a Professor from Cambridge University commented that its contents were "as marvelous and fascinating as the Great Steppe" and afterwards, key figures in the field of historical studies started listening to my point of view. I very much appreciate the opinion of Zhaken Taymaganbetov, Dean of History at the Kazakh National University who cannot find fault in the historical worth of my findings.

As for Mathematics, I sometimes feel that I have betrayed this science. Being one of several leading mathematicians in Kazakhstan, I have added my own bright chapter to the chronicles. The two important theorems of three new academics have now been established in the history of that science: one devised by two Europeans; Karter and Keller and the other, by the Kazakh, Zakiryanov.

And now I want to say a few words about original sources, which were once only available to professional historians. At present all are in print, including "The Secret History of the Mongols" written in 1240 by an unknown author, and are therefore accessible to anyone. I found "The Collection of Chronicles" by Rashid-Ad-Din, (1305), especially useful but with one distinction: the historians took one strand of information from it but I discovered another..

Finally, I am now approaching sixty and have already lived the best years of my life. There is no need for me to invent or exaggerate the value of anything, for I am a realist by nature. At the very least, I hope I done my people proud: I've returned Genghis Khan to the Kazakhs, placing him within the context of my belief in, and knowledge of, the great history of my ancestors.

CRIMINAL INTEREST IN THE SPORTS ACADEMY

I was the founder of the Academy of which I am now the Director. When I first arrived, it was still known as the Institute of Physical Education and looked more like the Augean stables than a place of higher education. Krymbek Kusherbayev, Minister of Education, with whom we later became good friends even said: "I wouldn't blame you for feeling offended: You have been appointed Principal of the capital's Unversity but are expected to manage a farmyard!"

Today our Academy is a private enterprise of which our shareholders own eighty percent. We required a lot of money and support towards the necessary acquisition of a large stock of equipment, gymnasiums and a stadium and I had no family money to fall back on: I was the son of a foreman of a collective farm in Hayrulla, not the nephew of some great business magnate and although I have powerful friends who offered their assistance, it was up to me to raise the funds.

I had been the Principal for only six months before the organisation went public but since 1998 I had been involved in the implementaion of a government decree on the reorganization of the Institute into the Kazakh Academy of Sport and Tourism as a joint-stock company during my three years' service in the Presidential department of Administration. My new post provided me with greater autonomy in decisions concerning the development of the Academy but this also brought high risks and all could have been lost. There had been cases where other respected and influential Principals had failed to protect the statuses of their universities, including the famous National Institute of Economics and the less well known Railway Academy, resulting in their being taken over by wealthier organisations.

The Sports Academy is probably the only institution of higher education that has not been bought out by oligarchs and the ruling upper circles but we have had to battle for ten long years to preserve its status.

No fewer than twenty four cases were lodged against me: such was the determination of those who wished to defame and charge me with criminal offences. In order to build a case for my defence, I familiarised myself with current legal legislation and acquired an in - depth knowledge of each of the Criminal and Civil Codes to hone my awareness of all of the pitfalls connected to national jurisprudence.

Nothing of this kind had happened at Ust-Kamenogorsk but the situation in Almaty was altogether different: the Academy owned a number of highly coveted sites in the town centre and every rich and powerful developer and in particular the city akims, were eager to use the land for their own benefit.

Some of those who opposed me were good acquaintances and I tried to explain the gravity of the situation by telling them: "I will give you the shirt off my back but if you take the Academy to pieces, how will we be able to provide our students, potentially the Olympic champions of the future, with the necessary training facilities? In some cases this argument had an effect, and in others quite the contrary.

It's worth mentioning here, a case concerning the Kazakh National University. The Head of the State dismissed the Principal on the grounds that he had sold off 34 hectares of land belonging to the University and at the time, no-one questionned the fact that he might have done so under force. Today, the land is occupied by a Marriott hotel and a large shopping centre...

I always asked Marziya for advice before making any important decision and each time she replied: "If you are removed from your post, you still have brains, your health and the support of your family. We'll find a solution and launch a new business".

I grew increasingly exhausted by my enemies' allegations and therefore welcomed the meeting of the Academic Council in 2000 which would determine an outcome once and for all. Forty statements were presented: an unprecedented number at an event of this kind. Twenty seven supported me but the thirteen who were opposed , were prepared to stop at nothing to have me dismissed from my post. Amongst those who had been invited to give statements was an undergraduate who, in her role as chair of the Committee for Matters Concerning Young Persons, had visited me on a regular basis. Unfortunately, she had somehow been persuaded to lodge false accusations against me for sexual harrasment and it was only afterwards, that Marziya learned from one of the vice-principlals' wives that this poor girl had been taken to a house in the country and forced to write this letter.

I taped the hearing of the Academic Council so that Marziya could listen to it. She may have harboured some doubts about my fidelity, perhaps thinking that "there's no smoke without fire", but she stood by me and when she learnt that this girl was from the same region as her, , even joked that I was consistent at least, in my good taste!

A month after this extraordinary hearing had taken place, I bumped into Sveta and asked her "Why did you do it?" The student, with eyes downcast, told me that she would come to see me soon with an explanation and an apology: I'm still waiting...

Thanks to the efforts of my deputies, many people regarded me as odious and during a press conferences one journalist asked: "It's rumoured that your female students were victims of harassment . What are your comments on this?" It seemed futile to waste time on excuses so adopting the tone of his enquiry, I replied: "If I had any problem in satisfying my lust, there are plenty of places where I could pay for it."

My wife's support in my role as Principal was not confined to her unshakable faith in my innocence. Once, when I was away on business, masked men arrested documents and cash from the accounts department. My mobile phone had no signal and so my anxious staff called Marziya for advice which she duly and calmly delivered from her wheelchair.

In those days, the Head of the tax police was Rakhat Aliyev but the person who dealt with my case was Amanchi Akpaev, the now deceased and former President of the Olympic Committee of Kazakhstan; a powerful man well equipped to deal with instigating change.

I learned to my cost, the working methods of this "Sports General".

When I was appointed Principal, he as President of the Football Federation invited me twice to become a member of this organization and join the executive committee. Then when we were reorganized as a joint-stock company, he changed his allegiance and sought instead, the support of R.Aliyev, the higher ranking Chair of our company's Board of Directors in an attempt to transfer ownership of our Masanchi street stadium to the Football Federation. The proposal was, and remains, non-negotiable.

Who or what gave me the strength to take on these powerful players: what was my motivation? I obviously wanted to retain my post as Principal but as a well-qualified mathematician, I would always be able to earn my living elsewhere. I am still seeking an answer to this question.

In the early 2000's, it seemed like the ministers of education were changed as often as women change their clothes. Regardless of whether they were in post for three years or only one year, each one would try to dig up the dirt on me.

I remember calling on Byrganym Aitimova to congratulate her a week after she had taken up office. After an exchange of courtesies I warned our new minister that she would soon be sent a poison letter about me. Smiling, she told me that she had received this information on her second day!

Inquiries abounded from senators, deputies, majilismen and ministers to the President on why the country's only sports institution operated on a shareholder basis. The then Minister of Internal Affairs, Zautbek Turysbekov, took a personal interest in our "Gorelnik" stadium, located behind the Medeo skating-rink. One day he invited me round for the *beshbarmak* (a Kazakh national dish) and although it was unacceptable to refuse an invitation from a man of such rank, I refused to go. As a result, documents concerning the stadium were forged and I was charged with a criminal offence. Fortunately, the General Prosecutor's Office made a stand for me and following the submission of a notice of appeal before the Supreme Court, the stadium was returned to the Academy. At that time I also received invaluable support from Senator Oralbay Abdykarimov who managed the anti-corruption commission under the "Nur Otan" People's Democratic Party. He facilitated a journalistic investigation which led to the break of the story behind the occupancy of the Academy's tourist base by Turysbekov's relatives.

Corruption is a reality of our country but there are honest authorities able to withstand this degradation. An example of this is illustrated by the involvement of Oralbai Abdykarimov when I appealed to him for support regarding further dispute at the Academy following an inquiry addressed to Yuriy Khitrin, the Attorney General of the Republic, and to Kairbek Suleymenov, Minister of Internal Affairs.

I had neither the desire nor the means to hire an investigator, prosecutor or judge, and I didn't have the backing of patrons with whom I could have shared my grievances over the lawlessness which surrounded me.

I drew my strength from some subconscious level and I must confess that during these trials, I turned from atheist to tangriist, convinced in my belief in *arauhans*, the spirits of my ancestors.

My wife had always told me: "Since your intentions are pure, the *arauhans* will come to your rescue" and now I had a chance to experience this.

The religion of our ancestors focuses on the cyclicity of life. Today it is winter but everything will change with spring and trees the will blossom again. Today the river is shallow and frozen over but in spring it will be filled again. People, according to Tengriism, are also bound to nature's cycles. Our paths through life can be compared to leaves that fall in autumn and cover the trees again in spring: by connecting with the world of our ancestors, we can find ways of refreshing our lives And if you don't manage to succeed in one sphere of this life, there is always the next.. Tengriism calls for us to believe in ourselves and our land, and also in love.

A few words about my woman: Marziya inspires and supports me and I am indebted to her for everything that I have achieved. When she was diagnosed with cancer in Seoul, Marziya selflessly thanked God for allowing her the past twenty years to dedicate to her children.. And I echo her gratitude: had she died after the accident, no-one can imagine know different our lives would have been. Her role as mother to Baurzhan and Asel and as wife to me, have made us who we are today.

My children know that their mother's illness could take her from us at any moment but the ferocity with which she fights her disease in order to continue nourishing the lives of both them and her grandchildren, is appreciated and cherished as an example of how all us should lead our lives.

We want her to enjoy her life as long as possible and I've told her that she has to be here to see our eldest grandchildren Tamerlan and Arslan marry and then, in due course, nurse her great-grandchildren.

… She possesses an amazing ability to win over friends and fellow-thinkers and this has often proved advantageous when I've hit hard times.

I understand that only a minority of the tens of thousands of people who appeal to the Head of State, ever have their cases heard but for some reason, any which concerned me always reached his desk. Growing irritated, the President asked the then Minister of Education, Krymbek Kusherbayes, "If this person is so despicable, why are we still employing him?"

The Minister replied: "Nursultan Abishevich, he remains in post because he is both honest and one of our most highly professional Principals." Weary of the whole business, the President retorted: "Well, if you hold him in such high esteem then transfer him to another university: it is clear that he no longer has any rapport with his current team."

Undeterred, the Minister offered a counter argument in which he maintained his position that I was without doubt the best Principal for the Sports Academy , as substantiated by the fact that I had succeeded in providing real benefits to the government by instigating the foundation of training facilities for future champions. He explained how my moral purity had been illustrated on many occasions, not least in March 1995, when the country was undergoing a change of government and Mambetkaziev, the Minister of Education, was sidelined. As one of his most loyal disciples, I then took the unprecedented action of stepping back to enable my mentor to take up the reins of Principal of the University of East Kazakhstan.

His persuasive report paid off and as a consequence, the Head of State gave me his full support when in June 2010, I wrote him a letter about plans being made to massacre our academy, involving some quasi-legal, semi-criminal structures. The President instructed the Attorney General to assess the situation objectively and impartially and the outcome was an instruction for all stolen property to be returned to its legal holder. It was on this positive note that the whole era of dispute over the Kazakh Academy of Sports and Tourism drew to a close.

It brought me immense relief, especially since I had endured so much for so long, including episodes where our house would be searched at four in the morning, with my wife lying sick in her room.

If it hadn't been for Marziya, the stress would have proved too much and I might have given up and let them have their way. Faced with similar situations, many other Principals had been coerced into agreeing with the oligarchs' demands in exchange for pay-offs but buoyed by my wife's determination to see justice done, I was able to continue fighting.

Both then and now I clearly recognized that things would have turned out quite differently, had I not ceded my post as Principal in the University of East Kazakhstan to my mentor in 1995. Linked to the subsequent chain of events are the support and friendship from Krymbek Kusherbaev, Imangali Tasmagambetov, one of our Republic's most remarkable people, and the Head of State, Nursultan Nazarbaev.

I have often wondered why I acted in one way rather than another and have come to realize that most of the time; my behaviour is rooted in my upbringing which instilled self-worth as well as loyalty towards people and principles.

This attitude has served me well. When Amangeldy Bektemisov, held the office of akim in the East Kazakhstan region, everyone tried to curry favour with him but as soon as the President appointed someone else, he was forgotten. I was one of the very few who continued to support him when he was in the lurch. Later, during a visit to Almaty, Minister Erejep Mambetkaziev, founder and first Principal of the East-Kazakhstan State University, called Bektemisov: "Amangeldy, I want you to come, Kairat is here". The three of us had a good time together and Bektemisov proposed a toast, the words of which I remember well: "Do you remember", he said addressing Mambetkaziev, "that when you were appointed Minister, you proposed that Kairat took your place as Principal and I opposed it on the grounds that he was too young and had too little experience to take charge Kazakhstan's largest University? I couldn't have been more wrong: I failed to see that behind his youth, he had the maturity of a man. I should have recognized his qualities since after all; he was the only person who remained loyal to me after I had lost my post."

ONE WEDDING RING FOR TWO
(A dialogue between two lovers)
LIFE IN NOVOSIBIRSK:
Marziya

After graduating from University we stayed in the capital. I was assigned to the computer centre at the Kazakh SSR State Planning Committee and Kairat began his PhD course at the Pedagogical Institute. Putting it lightly, his thesis supervisor was a little too old and so, on the enthusiastic recommendation of our friend Vitaliy Bloshitsin, Kairat decided to transfer to Novosibirsk.

I fully supported his decision since mathematical science had progressed much further in Novosibirsk than at our University. He was formally allocated as his thesis supervisor Asan Taimanov, Kazakhstan's guru of mathematical science, but his actual supervisor was Valery Avdeevich Churkin, a true Siberian and a wonderful man in all respects.

In the meantime, I was to stay in Almaty by myself and Kairat hastily found me a room in Tastak, moved me in and then left. The owners of this apartment turned out to be alcoholics and so were their friends and every night when I got home from work, I would lie trembling in fear as I listened to their drunken ravings. In desperation, after they had tried to break into my room, I called my classmates who immediately gathered both me and my belongings and drove me through the rain to stay at one of their homes. Having nowhere else to go, I then moved into my sister's room at her Halls of Residence.

During that period, Kairat and I could only dream of having a flat together in Almaty and never imagined that one day we would build our own houses in one of the city's best districts.

Things got even worse when the drunken landlord of one of our rented apartments let himself in with his own key and stole Kairat's wedding ring. At the time, I blamed my husband with the words: "God has punished you because you didn't want to wear that ring!" Later, on our 25th wedding anniversary, my own ring was made into two rings and since then, he has never taken it off!

But returning to the subject of accommodation: The Chairman of the State Planning Commission where I worked happened to be a good friend of Kairat's uncle on his mother's side. As soon as I had been enlisted to this department, our kindly Halit-aga offered to assist us with housing. He called me in and I hoped and expected that he would find us at least a room in one of the Halls, which was the general rule for young specialists. It was a damp cold day when I arrived for the meeting but his assistant was unwilling to show me into the Chairman's office despite my explanations that I had an appointment. Having waited all day for nothing, I felt like a dog which had been kicked and decided there and then that I would leave for Novosibirsk. The data centre's director didn't want to let me go, warning me: "As a young professional, you will be throwing away all of your prospects". I, in turn, responded: "And if I don't go, I'll be throwing away my family."

I took to life in the academic town of like a duck to water. I was employed by the Software Systems Research Institute and found it easy to master all manners of programming: Algol, COBOL, Assembler and FORTRAN.

I liked the atmosphere of this academic town which suited my nature and within two years I had made really good friends in Galka Kulichkova, Petrovich and Yurka Scheglov. We had a lot of fun together and the whole gang would regularly go off on picnics. I usually cooked cabbage pies for both these open-air lunches and for my colleagues in the laboratory and people constantly asked how I, the maker of such delicious puffy pies, could stay so slim!

Living here changed both my and Kairat's perspectives on life and enabled us to expand our horizons. We became a part of an environment in which everyone was keen on literature and tried to keep up to date with all new publications. Sheshe sent us books from Temir and Kairat was a regular customer of second-hand booksellers.

Kairat arranged for me to share a room with some female graduates in Almaty and then, when one of them moved on, we were allocated our own room. However, we still found ourselves being moved every two or three months and fed up; we even attempted to bribe the commandant. It didn't work and we were kicked out!

Kairat and I could only spend time together when our room mates were out or studying in the library but despite living in different halls and being without our son, we still felt very much a family.

WE ARE ECHOES OF EACH OTHER

Marziya

Today our lives are so intertwined that we can't live without each other for even a single moment. Kairat, for instance, never sits down at the table without me, although he can be very impatient when hungry. When we go abroad with our friends and they spend too much time at the shops, he gets impatient and is always the first in the restaurant.

Sometimes if I'm running around the outskirts of the city in search of building materials for his Academy, he'll call and ask "Where are you? It's lunchtime". I'll then drop everything and rush home, negotiating my way through the heavy traffic. In the evenings if I'm late, the children will sit down at the table but Kairat will always excuse himself, saying: "I'll wait for mum".

Kairat

The relationship between my parents was almost as close as ours. Father died in 1991, and whenever I visited my native Karakul, I would find my mother in a state of grief. She would say: "I wish the Almighty would take me into heaven soon; I want to be with your father". "What are you talking about, mother?!" I would reply in indignation "Enjoy life and the achievements of your children and your many grandchildren. Let's travel somewhere." "No, no," - she protested. – "I have only one desire now: to go to a better world."

Marziya

It was the same in my family. My lovely grandma, filled with grief after the death of my grandfather, sat in the corner pulling at her hair and shedding silent tears. She outlived him by only two and a half years. During that time she managed to nurse my son. She loved Baurzhan very much.

Father died at an early age and my mother who was still a young woman, could have embarked upon a new life. Instead, she concentrated wholeheartedly on her responsibilities to her children. She has recently passed away and it feels so sad and lonely without her in my heart even though I myself became a grandmother a long time ago.

Kairat

As a new graduate I only earned seventy eight rubles per month, fifty of which went on the rent for the apartment. Marziya didn't work since she had a small child to bring up. I was therefore very grateful to Marziya's mother Sheshe, when she took me to a store in Temir and bought me a whole new wardrobe of shoes, jacket, trousers, coat… She worked in a bookstore, and we very much enjoyed visiting her at work. In the city, books could only be acquired from catalogues and with coupons but here there was an enormous selection. We gathered dozens of volumes and her mother sent us more through the post. We transported them from apartment to apartment in Almaty: we had almost no possessions, only hundreds of volumes of scientific literature and fiction.

Marziya

Kairat spent a lot of time reading so it was up to me to run the house. However, whenever he was free, he was always willing to help and did it well! If I was chopping onions, he would peel the potatoes and whilst I washed the dishes, Kairat would vacuum.

At the Vostokkazgeologiya computer centre where I worked, all of the programmes were printed on paper punch cards. The dust caused the skin on my hands to swell and in addition I developed a severe allergy to washing powder. Aware of the situation, Kairat took over the laundry and I never had to do it again.

Later, when Aselka was born and Kairat was away for four months in Novosibirsk finishing his Ph.D. thesis, the baby's nappies were washed by my brother Sultan, a maths student at Ust-Kamenogorsk Pedagogical Institute. It happened that I had paved the way for all of my brothers and sisters, persuading each of them to study maths. Our school in Temir had also played a part in their career choices, since it employed an excellent maths and physics teacher named Yurii Kastygin, and all of our family had scientific minds.

So as I was saying, Kairat never shied away from household tasks and was comfortable and happy to be seen helping me out in communal areas of the Halls. And thus we have been supporting each other in even the simplest things throughout our lives together.

However, if I ever asked Kairat to fix a curtain rail or an iron or a cooker, he would explode! I found this strange since my father, uncles and brothers were all skilled at repairing and taking apart and re-assembling anything mechanical, from bikes to cars and indeed, were so good at it that everyone in town would call upon them for assistance. My man however, was simply not very practical and his inability would make him angry and irritable. Once I had accepted that he quite simply, didn't have any inert technical skills I took charge of this area. To this day, he prefers to keep his distance from anything of this sort: I even have to configure his mobile phone!

In short, my husband is a pure theorist with practical skills restricted to pen and paper. But luckily, my son Baurzhan takes after the menfolk of my family and takes great pleasure in playing about with the engine of the Mercedes!

Kairat

When Kazakhs began to divide themselves according to their origins, a saying emerged: give the staff to a Kazakh from the First zhuzh and send him to graze sheep; to a Kazakh from the Middle zhuzh, give a pen and send him to debate, and give a spear and a battlefield to a Kazakh from the Third zhuzh. In other words, the First zhuzh are cattlemen and shepherds, the Middle, are thinkers, scientists and philosophers, and the Third are warriors. I turned out a hostage of the Middle zhuzh. I may be no handyman, but I have many other capabilities. The word *orta* (middle) also means "central", a word I believe to be better suited to the concept of *zhuzh*.

Marziya

We complement each other perfectly. Kairat is a great tactician and strategist, whilst I by referencing life experiences, am quickly able to weigh up and analyze the consequences and then calculate what should be done.

As a married couple we have always shared our thoughts and exchanged knowledge on what we've seen or read and I found that I was usually able to find a solution to problems over which Kairat had been puzzling for some time.In short, I am good at solving strategic problems but have neither the time nor patience to explore tactics.

That is why most of what happens in our family is based on my desires but realized by Kairat: thanks to my strategies and his tactics, we have managed to deal honourably with even in the most testing situations.

ENVY AND JEALOUSY ARE BLOOD SISTERS

Kairat

I recall a recent incident when I was sitting in a meeting of the Organizing Committee for the Winter World University Games 2017 under the chairmanship of Prime Minister Serik Akhmetov. At the end of the meeting we were asked to read over proposals for events and I noticed that there was no mention of the Student Sports Federation of Kazakhstan, the alma mater of which is the Kazakh Academy of Sports and Tourism.

All the medals had been made and the roles of representatives of the various organizations had been already been determined so it was too late to honour the institution which having paved the way for the whole event, had been conveniently "forgotten." . At the same time everybody knew that if I, as Chairman of the Federation hadn't initiated and realized the project, Almaty would never have become the capital of the World Student Games.

Taking a philosophical stance, I recalled an old parable. The Khan of one of the belligerent states found himself in a very difficult situation but an ordinary soldier came to the rescue and the army returned home victorious.

The soldier boasted to everyone about how he had saved the Khan's life but was furious that the Khan hadn't thanked him properly. Aggrieved, he went to the khan's quarters, where he was duly rewarded with flocks of sheep and horses. However, on the way home, was murdered by the Khan's assassins.

What is the moral of this tale? I have learnt that there is no value in my retaliating every time my achievements are undermined or unacknowledged, if I then, metaphorically speaking, end up being beaten up and left lying in the bushes like that hapless soldier.

At that meeting, I took the floor and advised the Prime Minister and members of the Government about the problem concerning the Student Sports Federation and how it could be addressed. As a result, it was agreed that we would attend the Student World Championships with a guarantee of a bonus of 50,000 dollars for taking first prize in the Games. It more than proved that I was fit for my job and I was even happier when a Principal of another University who was attending the same meeting, whispered to me: "Kairat-aga, you have given the city a tremendous gift; Kaztransgas is laying a gas pipeline to cater for the Student Games and money from the national budget has been allocated for the construction of new thermal power stations, the airport, transport interchanges and student accommodation. In addition, each regional centre is to have modern sports facilities for children and adolescents".

Marziya

I felt sad when I noticed a shadow of envy amongst our closest friends when we achieved our long awaited success. Anyone who knows us will agree that Kairat and I will always fight unsparingly to defend something we believe in but it seemed that in this case, they found it easier to sympathize with our efforts than congratulate us on realizing our goal. This is something that I've grown used to but since we ourselves are always sincerely happy with other people's hard-earned success, I still find it difficult to understand why some people can't share others' joy.

Perhaps, when they read these words, some of our friends will be prompted to question their own consciences.... On reaching thirty, I learned with relief, that nasty attacks of envy are extrinsic to me and I even remember the place where I made this discovery: my beloved country house where I would often take time to reflect on life.

The City Executive Committee of Ust-Kamenogorsk allocated us a much discussed six acre plot of land on rocky, pertain terrain. Kairat, Baurzhan and I tilled this land by hand to expose the fertile soil and our hard work paid off each autumn. Thinking about the almost indescribable beauty of the surrounding landscape later helped me cope with the pain and dark thoughts which struck me after the accident. The neighbouring land was owned by Kairat's colleagues and because the soil was a little better and they had more disposable income, they were able to lay down a water supply and build their country house quite quickly.

Despite spending every spare moment working our land, we had to wait much longer until we could begin building but we accepted our limitations and never envied our neighbours.

Envy and jealousy are blood sisters. I wasn't jealous of Kairat, but sometimes I felt a slight gnawing at my heart when he was over enthusiastic in his attentions to young women. And then imagining how this feeling could easily be extended towards other more materialistic aspects of our lives, I was very glad that I really wasn't by nature, a jealous or envious sort.

People who are shackled by envy or jealousy lead complicated and embittered lives and their powers of reason are weakened: in short, their road through life can only lead to a dead end. I pity anyone who finds themselves in this desperate state and often think about that man in a wheelchair whose resentment towards healthy people was so strong that he couldn't bear to look at them and even wished them dead.

Kairat

There have been several occasions when I have felt that it would be better to be dead than alive.

The first time was at the scene of the accident when my chest felt so tight that I could barely breathe and I was suffering from severely painful head injuries. If I had had a gun, I could have shot myself.

The second event occurred in 2005. I was bathing in the sea in the Philippines and stepped on a stonefish: the most poisonous creature in the world with a bite ten times stronger than that of a scorpion. The pain, focused on one part of the body, drives you mad and whilst we were speeding to shore in a motorboat, I felt like jumping onto the blades of the propeller. The only thing that stopped me was the guarantee that death by this "meat-grinder" wouldn't have been instantaneous. Just before I lost consciousness, I called Marziya in Almaty.

When I was discharged from hospital a day later, the Philippine doctor told the doctor from our team: "He's a lucky guy: there have been around five hundred fatal bites by these fish." I probably owe my survival to the Almighty and Marziya's prayers.

The last time I felt that I wanted to die was during one summer when I was a post graduate in Novosibirsk. I lay in delirium for three days after a tick bite but luckily, Marziya had come to visit me with Aselya and nursed me back to health.

… The Almighty has sent me and Marziya many tests. Now we are facing another challenge and I pray to God and the aruahs to help us and our family.

Marziya

The first person I saw after a prolonged period of unconsciousness in intensive care was Kairat with a bandaged head. He asked: "What can I get you to eat?" And I didn't want anything apart from the brown book of Tyutchev poetry, which I still have, and my make-up. I felt completely washed out and wanted to put on a little powder and lipstick.

Kairat

Marziya attends clinics on a regular basis and a nurse once remarked: "We have many women walking in here on their own two feet but not all of them bother about their personal hygiene. You on the other hand, are always so beautifully presented and emanate an aroma of cleanliness. You are an incredible woman!"

I chose Marziya above all of the other girls because I felt that she would be a good wife and mother of my children. Neatness and cleanliness are important in every aspect of her life. Sometimes I can get irritated by with her obsession with always being fragrant and perfectly groomed, and implore: "You're at home by yourself and we aren't expecting guests, so why do you need to take three showers a day?!"

But this is just the way she is and she'll never change.

Marziya

My Kazakh grandparents were very fastidious people. Even when religion was banned, they still performed namaz and abolitions five times a day and there was always a pitcher of water in lavatory.

Striving to maintain cleanliness was natural in my family. We didn't have our own bath, so visited the city bathhouse once a week, and in the interim, water was heated in a large cauldron outside the house and adults would first wash themselves and then the children. In summer, grandfather bathed in the river, whatever the weather. The house always had to be immaculate otherwise, as the eldest child; I would be in deep trouble.

Despite the acute shortage of water, my grandparents refused to drink any water which had collected in a bucket within five metres of the basin. They called such water *aram-su* or foul water, and gave it to the cattle.

Family values have an invaluable impact upon a child's character and if these are reinforced at school, the child will be well prepared for the future. Nowadays, life skills are no longer taught in classrooms and it's a pity that teachers have so little involvement in the spiritual development of children.

Even the youngest of my grandchildren will pay attention to me when I have something important to say and they are always willingly to discuss things with me. This was well illustrated by the eldest, Tamerlan, when he was only eight years old. Carelessly, I had once spurted out in his presence: "I guess I'm going to die, there's no way I'm going to survive this." Alarmed, and looking quickly at his father, my boy cried: "No, Apa: don't die! If you die, who will teach us how to do things properly?"

He was too young to understand what death is but was nevertheless worried: "How am I going to live without Apa?" My grandson is now 16 years old but I will never forget these words: they express exactly my position in the family, and indeed to friends, as someone who was always there to offer support and guidance.

Ever observant Tamoska says of me: "She will offer advice to anybody". My analytical mind allows me to quickly assess a situation which then leads to a "diagnosis" but of course, I would never assume to instruct: "do this, and all will be well". Instead, I will usually offer: "I think that this is the way to go, but you should decide for yourself."

This is how I was brought up: both my grandparents and parents had encouraged me to voice my opinions ever since I was a small girl and would ask: "Mzeken, and what do you think?" By respecting each other's points of view, regardless of their age, no-one ever had to raise their voice to be heard and this is something I have instilled in my grandchildren.

The great Socrates said something along the lines of: "Start speaking and I will know you" but my grandparents didn't need to read the philosopher to follow this doctrine which sustained them and in turn, me, through any blows that life threw at us.

I was brought up surrounded by fine literature, both poetry and prose and I admire Lermontov, even more than Pushkin. It amazes me how someone who lived for only twenty seven years, produced such profoundly philosophical work.

Waiting up for Kairat to return home late from work I unvoluntarily recalled one of Lermontov's most poignant poems in which he appeals to his beloved after she had waved him aside. Shuddering with pain and in tears I repeated the lines, so consonant with my feelings:

I shall not stoop before you.
Neither thy greeting, nor thy reproach
Has control over my soul.
Be aware that we are strangers from now on.

Whenever I felt that my husband had treated me unjustly, I became so angry that I didn't just weep into my pillow; I also used to punch it so hard that clouds of dust reached the ceiling. We have such fierce arguments that it's a wonder that we're still together. It's probably because we never dispute anything which springs from our consciences. We don't have much money but people believe us to be in funds because we are never economical when it comes to nourishing our souls.

In the summer of 2011, after breaking a leg on holiday Turkey, I began to experience regular health problems. Kairat was worried about me and had we been able to afford it, we would have gone to Israel to get treatment for my sores. Instead, I had no alternative but to attend the clinic in Kalkaman where Doctor Bekishev is the only doctor in Kazakhstan who treats sores with bakteriphages (immunobiological preparations with antibacterial action). I was discharged within just two weeks and told that a doctor would visit me at home. My paralysis, severe sores and diabetes, rendered my condition potentially fatal and basically, the clinic did not want their reputation marred by a the death of a patient.

To counter our despair and the sudden threat to my life expectancy, Kairat arranged to have a documentary made about my life. He contracted a director and gathered up our children, family and friends to participate in filming first in my homeland and then, in his.

Later on, when Asel expressed her dissatisfaction with the quality of the documentary, her father indgnantly retorted: "I ordered the film as a memorial to your mother. She was dying! How dare you criticize me!"

Kairat always says that he fell in love with me at first sight and this love has never faded. Now, after chemotherapy, my head looks like an egg. I waited for Kairat to return from work before I shaved off my remaining tufts of hair but I have no doubt that after thirty seven years of marriage, my soul is more important than my hair. Of course, there was a time at the very beginning when things were rather different and he stopped loving me for a moment after I'd had my hair cut too short!

TOGETHER FOR LIFE

Kairat
I managed to capture her heart.

Marziya
And swept me up from under the noses of all of my suitors! Three of them had proposed marriage but he was the one who counquered me!

WAS OUR TRAGEDY CONDUCIVE TO MY CAREER?

Kairat
Heaven forbid that I should think about making connections between successes in my career with our misfortune, but if the accident hadn't happened in August 1991, I probably wouldn't be where I am today and would never have realized my true potential. The severe tests on my morality arrested the attention of numerous people, including our country's most eminent leaders, and ironically, helped rather than hindered my career path.

Until the day of the accident, I was an unbeliever but I now feel that because I lived by high morals, I was rewarded by the Almighty.

After receiving Marziya's last diagnosis, I decided it was time to relieve myself of some of my responsibilities and so although I remain President of our joint-stock company, the Principal's position is now occupied by our son: Baurzhan Kairatovich Zakiryanov. He has studied in Europe, has recently submitted his Ph.D. thesis and is now in charge of all current internal affairs. When transferring the reins of power to him, I told my son: "It is up to you how you manage the students and lecturers and determine the course syllabuses and qualifications. That will leave me to deal with external matters concerning the development of the Academy and allow me to focus on your mother's health."

I don't know how much time we have but in the name of my love for my wife, I will try to do everything in my power to prolong Marziya's life.

Marziya

Fate rendered me disabled but mercifully and in tandem with my family's unfailing support, also gave me the beautiful gift of over twenty more years of life.

When, in autumn 2012, the doctors pronounced my death sentence, our university friends offered their condolences to us both, explaining that since they had always regarded Kairat and me as one complete unit, any pain inflicted on me must equally affect him.

My sister offered to find me a psychotherapist but I told her that she would be better trying to find one for my family who had been propelled into a state of relentless panic.

In order to somehow console my relatives and cease their endless tears, I had to promise that I wasn't going to die any time soon and would do my best, as I always had, to struggle on. All they needed to do was support me.

I once read a desperate letter posted by a guy on the Internet which asked: "Is it possible to live with a spinal fracture?"

I wrote telling him that I had the same diagnosis and advised: "If you pull yourself together, you can learn how to deal with it. My children were 15 and 10 years old, when I broke my spine and now that they have grown up and established their own families, I have five wonderful grandchildren. Until very recently, I was actively engaged in the construction business but most importantly, managed to keep my family and husband close beside me.

Despite being wheelchair-bound, I have travelled halfway around the world, bathed in all the seas and oceans and never missed a single family holiday or a picnic arranged for friends .Everything is in your hands and everything depends on your frame of mind.

Of course, you'll have more challenges ahead of you than most able-bodied people but you can train your body to cope without assistance. I'm not denying that it is difficult but if you take deep breathes instead of whining, and resist the temptation of drowning your despair in alcohol; you'll find that a joyful life awaits you."

I don't dwell on the negatives and am practical and rational by nature, but I am equally, very romantic and optimistic, and that might be the reason why my husband still makes a fuss over me.

HERE'S TO HAPPINESS

As Kozma Prutkov used to say, if you want to be happy, then be happy. So here I am: I wanted to be happy and I became happy. Victories over your own weaknesses are the hardest but they repaid me generously: I was practically helpless yet managed to make people recognize me for the person I am, rather than a dependent invalid. Like anyone else, I could have easily chosen to cast aside make-up and manicures and gone about *au natural* but this was never my style and once disabled, I made all the more effort with my appearance. There's a spirit within me that won't allow me to be considered worse off than anyone else and luckily, I receive no pity from friends and relatives. My husband even goes so far as to tell me that my positive attitude helps my nearest and dearest to believe in themselves.

Love lies at the heart of believing in oneself but it needs to be nurtured. Once after St. Valentine's Day I had a conversation with my assistant Abay and Gaziz, Kairat's driver. I asked the boys: "How did you celebrate with your sweethearts? I hope you didn't forget flowers". When they confessed that they limited themselves to phone calls, I was filled with indignation and implored them: "How many times have I told you that feelings, as well as things, need to be taken care of?! If neglected, they will gradually disintegrate and disappear and you and your wives will end up living like neighbours instead of lovers. My husband, who is almost 60 years old, didn't get home from work until midnight but still managed to buy me flowers".

To outsiders, it may appear that the close bounds which my family share, my husband's career and the success of our children, came naturally but all were due to continuous hard work, care and attention. If for example, I was ever unable to serve breakfast to my husband, I would ensure that I provided an explanation: "Honey, I'm unwell, please have breakfast without me today then kiss me goodbye."

Living under the same roof for thirty seven years, Kairat and I have always slept together and it surprised me to hear that many of our friends, who are couples, have separate bedrooms. Whenever, my nervous system feels particularly tense and I am restless, I find that holding my husband's hands in sleep, makes me feel calmer and more relaxed. I agree when people advocate that couples should maintain the intimacy of their youth in order for their marriage to remain safe and sincere.

What is love after all? In the beginning it is bound up in physiology and the instinct to procreate but that hormonal rush doesn't last forever and that is why so many young people find themselves in trouble before too long and if they decide to part after having children, then these young innocents effectively become the orphans of living parents.

Much can be said in praise of parental advice as well as literature and even the cinema, as providers of guidelines concerning married life and one's choice of a life partner.

Kairat often repeats that love is like an illness which affects the mind and soul but in me he was able to see not just a young pretty girl, but a good wife and a loyal friend. And I, when he placed his heart at my feet, didn't push away this explosive, snooty, and sometimes even flamboyant boy, even though there were times when I could easily have walked away after one of his showdowns!

And we, to everyone's surprise, became the almost perfect couple, completing each other.

In difficult moments I inspire both him and all of my relatives, by citing the epithet that has belonged to my clan since their early days as warriors: Never be afraid and all will be well. Nothing is impossible for someone who seeks truth."

After all, how did my husband emerge victorious from even the most alarming situations? I know how to analyze a situation, and Kairat, armed with a new understanding of the situation as well as knowledge of both the individuals concerned and the rules of the game, puts it all into practice. For example, when he campaigned to save the Academy, I advised him to risk all by fighting in the public arena and told him: "You are an honest man, so you make your notions transparent to all and then let your opponents try to challenge you against this background".

Of course, in this case, much time needed to evaluate the human psychology involved and at many stages, things definitely hung in the balance. Someone once said that Kairat had been born in a caul and I think that's true: he's been very lucky to have mustered the support of good people but ultimately, it's his purity that conquers even the most ardent enemies. I often ask myself, how it is that Kairat manages to win in situations where people with greater connections and means don't dare to even open their mouths. I think it stems from the way in which we as a family relates to one another: in any argument it is vital to put personal matters aside and focus only on the facts, but most importantly, to be able to rely on someone close to you. People usually break "under the pressure" not because they are weak but because their power diminishes as soon as they are betrayed by those on whom they depend for support.

Kairat's love makes me a strong and self-confident woman. Now I have no hair at all yet my husband says that in his eyes, I'll always be beautiful. I think that he infects everyone around us with his love for me: when people hear my name on his lips and notice how Kairat's voice and facial expression change when he starts talking about me, they want to meet me.

Today my only regret is that I didn't have enough strength to advance my profession. Kairat comforts me by listing my achievements as a good wife, mother and grandmother, and latterly as a superintendent of building projects, but nevertheless, my working career didn't turn out the way I imagined it in my youth.

I wanted to be an important scientist but am happy and proud that my husband and children succeeded where I failed.

DON'T ASK FOR WHOM THE BELL TOLLS

Kairat Zakiryanov

It's now September 2013 and Marziya has been fighting the fourth stage of her cancer for almost a year. In the clinic in Seoul, she has received ten blasts of chemotherapy, the last five of which were double doses. Her doctor Professor Che is astonished by her powers of endurance, especially since her body is so weak. I believe that Marziya's book provides the reasons why.

I don't know how many more years or days God has granted her, but we thank Him for every moment given to our family. A few days ago we lost a dear family friend, Bagdat Shayahmetov. Words can't express the pain of our loss.

John Donne, the 16th century English poet expressed it well:

"No man is an island, entire of itself; every man is a piece of the Continent, a part of the main; if a clod be washed away by the sea, Europe is less, as well as a promontory were, as well as if a manor of thy friends or of thine own were; any man's death diminishes me, because I am involved in Mankind; And therefore never sad to know for whom the bell tolls; it tolls for thee."

This autumn, God willing, we will celebrate thirty eight years of our lives together. I recall the poignant words of V.Belinsky on love: "Love has its own laws of development; it ages like life itself. It has its own luxurious spring, followed by hot summers, and finally, autumn which can be warm, light and fertile for some but cold, barren and rotten for others".

Our autumn is very warm and filled with gratitude, and we would like it to be long in spite of the edicts of nature. The writer Agatha Christie once said: "I love this life. And no despair, misery and torments of hell will ever make me forget that it's a great blessing – just to live…" Marziya chose a slightly paraphrased expression by Tvardovsky for the title of her book: "Life over Pain and Despair". She loves this life so much; she loves me and her children, adores her grandchildren, eagerly awaits great-grandchildren and cares deeply for her friends and relatives. I pray to the Lord and aruahs: Don't take this worthy woman without your grace. Amen.

TWO TENDER VOLCANOES

Sergei Manakov, classmate

I was the best man at their wedding, and then their son's godfather. At the beginning, I and other fellow students often laughed and wondered how Kairat and Marziya, two volcanoes, could ever live together?! But they proved us all wrong by becoming inseparable.

As a couple they have sustained the friendship and loyalty of their youth through their lives together. Despite difficult circumstances, roaming from one apartment to another, Marziya always made her friends feel welcome, serving us her specialty dish of sausages with pasta.

It's been long since we all became grandparents, but when we gather in their house, we forget about our grey hair and widening girths and behave as if we were those same girls and boys who first met forty years ago. And it's Marziya who brings us together.

A MAN WITH THE SOUL OF A CHILD
AND THE HEART OF TEENAGER

Taksyn Mustafina, family friend

There are no laymen in my immediate circle: I find that I cannot be friends with people with whom I have nothing in common, even though I know I should. This is perhaps the reason that I gained a reputation for being incorruptible and why it was believed that the Zakiryanov "paid me off".

... For most of my life, I worked as the ordinary lecturer at the University of Physical Education. Initially, I turned down the post of Dean of the new faculty, inaugurated in the Academy of Sports and Tourism by Kairat Zakiryanov but was persuaded to change my mind by one of his colleagues. It was a decision I did not regret.

Prior to his appointment as Principal, I was ashamed of the poor reputation of the Institute but now feel proud to be part of this organization. I would describe Kairat Zakiryanov as a man with the open soul of a child and the heart of a teenager; the ardor and faith which he has invested in the organization is infectious and has boosted the morale and loyalty of all those who work for him.

I think that that accident was a test of his love to Marziya. Getting acquainted with the Principal at work, and then afterwards becoming family friend, I noticed that whenever Marziya is involved, Kairat Zakiryanov's voice changes and his face brightens. His love enables her to live with dignity, but she too puts in a lot of effort. She possesses many admirable qualities for which she is loved: her internal purity, her absence of envy and her ability to ensure that life around her runs smoothly and efficiently. On one occasion when I accompanied her husband home, Marziya apologized to Kairat that she had not had time to do something but he simply replied: "I don't want anything except to see you when I get in from work." Taking me aside, she then expressed one of her main concerns: "If something happens to me, what will happen to Kairat? Will he have a breakdown?"

It is understandable why some people with disabilities become embittered. Think about it: it takes at least a half of the day for someone who is confined to a wheelchair to get ready to go out, compared to the fifteen or twenty minutes spent by an able-bodied person. Yet, whilst there are times when I refuse invitations to events because I simply can't be bothered to think about what to wear etc. , Marziya always turns up impeccably groomed. She would never dream of relaxing her standards, believing that it can be all too easy to fall into the habit of not being prepared to make an effort.

Through my friendship with her, I learned to stop worrying about my own blood pressure and risks of a heart attack, shamed by the fact that only once did I hear her say: "I don't feel very well". During this phone call, I told her: "You're far too well to be complaining about being ill" and she laughed and replied "That's funny, coming from you, Taskyn Kurakovna!"

When I hung up, I was embarrassed about how tactless I had must have sounded but I also realized that I stopped noticing her disability some time ago…

MY APA IS MY HEROINE

Tamerlan Zakiryanov, grandson

No matter what happens she continues to work hard at making her dreams come true; probably because being so ill, she realizes that she may not have another chance.

I was a few years old when her friend, Basya, the Shar-Pei died. When

"Apa" (grandmother in Kazakh language)

aspashka returned from Talgar where she had buried her dog, it was clear that she was heartbroken but after spending about twenty minutes alone in her bathroom, she picked up the phone and immersed herself in organizing work at the construction site.

It was she who took charge of me during the first five years of my life: she could be very strict and exacting but no-one, not even my mother, spoiled me as much as she did. We often discussed the values of love and friendship and she impressed upon me the importance of using my intelligence and talents to achieve my goals. I have yet to reach my full potential but have done well in my sports and have already won several regional, and one Republican, competitions in mathematics.

THE CENTRE OF OUR SMALL UNIVERSE

Asel Artykova, daughter

For some reason my parents believe that their children's childhood, especially mine, was difficult. Foremost in my memories is the spiritual comfort which reigned in our house. My happy childhood wasn't clouded by endless housekeeping chores: As an eleven year old girl, I often managed to prepare salads and set the table for unexpected guests within a half an hour. Yet before the accident, I remember my mother being upset by the notion that her youngest child was growing up too pampered.

I recall one occasion when we were on a family holiday, immediately after my father's appointment as a Principal of the East Kazakh State University, waking up in tears. Mum and Dad rushed into my room: "What's wrong, dear?" And I answered: "I had a terrible dream that a bus arrived with an endless stream of visitors flowing out of it…"

In those days, guests visited our home constantly and it was necessary for us to welcome all of them, set the table and then clear up, well into the night. After my dream, father forbade his subordinates from visiting us at home.

We follow a tradition of celebrating our "family's birthday" on October 30 (the day my parents got married) every year. I see father and mother growing closer and closer to each other with every passing year. Mum has had to go through a lot, but she has always done so with great dignity. Due to my father's support – he had always been a tower of strength for her- the family is today inseparable.

I am so proud of my parents. Father's desire to "conquer the world" speaks of his acute and imaginative mind, but the centre of our little universe is our mother. Our house is but a shell without her.

MARZIYA IS LIFE

Pyotr Pominov, family friend,
Member of the Union of Journalists of the Kazakh Republic,
Philological Sciences candidate

I have been acquainted with Marziya for thirty years but now realize that I didn't really know her at all. I have her book in front of me and don't recall, despite being a professional philosopher, ever reading such a powerful work. It seems to me that even Dostoevsky with his raw realism didn't invest in his work, such intimate details. In the process of reading, certain questions arose in my mind and despite my knowledge of Marziya's legendary frankness I had to wonder: Why has such a strong willed woman found it necessary to publish the most intimate details of her life? So I sought the advice of my close friends and repeatedly referred to Dostoevsky to whom truth was equal to life itself. I also referenced my love for the words of Tvardovsky: "Life is more than war". Marziya writes with great conviction about how she molded (not forged, as some would argue) her victory in this war against her misfortune, hour by hour, day by day. Having been visited by suicidal thoughts, she was finally able to conclude: "Life can overcome misfortune". Marziya Zakiryanova's book triumphs life, love and happiness.

Of course, truth can heal and it can also harm. We should think carefully before we speak. I've never read literature like this before and through it, have become re-acquainted with the whole Zakiryanov family: Kairat's and Marziya's mighty clan. And my love for them has grown even stronger.

It is hard to believe that Marziya remembers the names of everyone she has ever met. This, of course, is a gift from God: such love of life and people. The author's Maximalism and frankness recall the golden age of 19th century Russian literature , I feel certain that a great destiny awaits this book and can only guess how many people will discover through it, a restoration of faith and love for life.

THANK YOU FOR THE HONOUR OF BEING YOUR FRIEND

Olga Kastygina, daughter of my teachers
Nadejda Ivanovna Chupik and Yuriy Nikolaevich Kastygin,
and my colleague in public projects

Marziya! I read the book avidly and couldn't stop until I had finished it. First of all, thank you for including me amongst your "close friends" whom you trusted to read this "confession": for this is how I regard this book which you and Kairat have written. Everything is described with cutting- edge frankness. There is no doubt that this book will prove invaluable , not only for your descendants but also for anyone looking for guidance in overcoming life's difficult circumstances with fortitude, truth to principles and LOVE with a capital "L" : everything which you

182

and Kairat lived by. I admire you, love you and pray to the Almighty to help you!

FORGIVE US ALL

Raufa Nazyrova, Kairat Zakiryanov's aunt

Marziya, I can't put into words, the feelings which arose in me while reading your book. I bow before your parents for their kindness, justice and for preparing you to deal with all of the hard knocks that have come your way.

Marziya, it is wonderful that you committed to paper your feelings and history to be shared with your loved ones and perhaps, the world at large. No one could remain indifferent to your fate after reading your book.

I would like to draw special attention to your mother-in-law, my sister. She was a very kind person with a generous soul but because of her personality, kept her feelings hidden. She avoided spoiling her children and only her youngest daughter, Sholpan, was given affectionate names – Sholtken, Sholtri, Issuri. But she was proud of you and was forever telling people about "our Marziya". We were very close to her, shared a lot with each other, and I knew that she loved and cared about you.

That fact that Kairat's parents lived in a distant province had an impact on their characters: they were somewhat naive and perhaps even a little ignorant. I am still surprised that we were able to break out of there and get an education. So please, forgive them if there's something in their lives that they did wrong. And forgive me, too. I wanted to write about so many things but seemed to have only expressed "sketchy" thoughts: words however, which are truly heartfelt.

CONTENTS